Śāṇḍilyasūtram

Śāṇḍilyasūtram

with the Commentary of Svapneśvara

translated by

Nandalal Sinha

Munshiram Manoharlal
Publishers Pvt. Ltd.

ISBN 81-215-0826-6
Second revised edition 1998
First published 1918

Typeset, printed and published by
Munshiram Manoharlal Publishers Pvt. Ltd.,
Post Box 5715, 54 Rani Jhansi Road, New Delhi 110 055.

Contents

Preface

The present work is based on the text edited by Ballantyne and published in the *Bibliotheca Indica*, new series, in 1861. The translation has been very much facilitated, and, in many places, considerably improved by E.B. Cowell's work published in the same series in 1878. Cowell's rendering has been found to be inaccurate in several places; yet we have not hesitated to borrow liberally from his footnotes which are very helpful, and from his translation of texts of reference where an improvement was not called for. We are glad to take this opportunity of acknowledging our great obligation to these two eminent Sanskrit scholars.

Nothing definite is known regarding the author or the date of the One Hundred Aphorisms of Śāṇḍilya. "They are the work of some anonymous teacher," according to Cowell, "who ascribed his doctrine to the ancient *ṛsi* Śāṇḍilya, partly because he wished to conceal its modern origin under a name belonging to Vedic times, and also because the Śāṇḍilya-vidyā supplied a convenient vantage-ground for his main doctrine of the necessity of faith." This theory must be rejected. The "doctrine of the necessity of faith" is not the anonymous teacher's own evolution. It has a very much older origin. In Cowell's language, "The name Śāṇḍilya is found in a well-known passage of the *Chāndogya Upaniṣad* (III.14), which recurs with a few verbal difference in the *Śatapatha Brāhmaṇa* (X.vi.3); the sage is there represented as declaring that the soul within us is Brahman. His doctrine is directly referred to in aphorism 31 of the present work, and the commentary quotes the passage from the *Chāndogya Upaniṣad*. This doctrine is called the Śāṇḍilya-vidyā in the *Vedāntasāra*, and it is there characterised as consisting of devotional meditations directed towards Brahman viewed as possessed of qualities rather than as the Absolute. The author of these aphorisms apparently accepts his view as the true. . . ." The doctrine was not "originally propounded in the *Bhagavadgītā*", as supposed by Cowell; "the history of the Hindu doctrine of faith (*bhakti*)" must be traced from the Vedic times.

The supposed antagonism of Knowledge and Devotion is another serious popular misconception. Ballantyne writes: "Śāṇḍilya rejects the Hindu (gnostic) theory that knowledge is the one thing needful, and contends that knowledge is only the handmaid of *faith*." Upon this Cowell comments: "Śaṅkara's view of knowledge is clearly expressed in the following passage of his commentary on the *Śvetāśvatara Upaniṣad,* which will serve to bring the two views into sharp contrast. "When men, disregarding the fruit, perform works only for the sake of *Īśvara*, these works become indirectly a means to liberation, as being a means for producing that purity of the internal organs which is a means to knowledge, which is the means to liberation." But Śaṅkara, more than any other reformer of his eminence, has been greatly misunderstood. Few have made any serious attempt to study his life and work as a whole. Śaṅkara must be studied not only in his commentaries on the Upaniṣads and the *Brahma-sūtras*, but also in his commentary on the *Gītā,* in his hymns, and in his daily life. He himself was one of the greatest *bhaktas* that ever lived on earth. A rich vein of the purest and highest Devotion runs through his hymns to the manifestations of Brahman such as Śiva, etc. In his commentary on the *Gītā,* VI.47, he explains that the person who worships Vāsudeva with faith is the wisest of the wise. Elsewhere he declares: "It is Devotion which is the greatest of all the means of Release." The consummation of Knowledge is in Devotion. The goal is the name, whether described as *sarvam khalu idam brahma* (All this verily is Brahman), or as *vāsudevaḥsarvam* (All is Vāsudeva). A sharp contrast is visible only when you do not look at the essentials, but at the temporary imperfections of the different environments of the beginners. One beginner is engaged in hearing the truths about Brahman from the teachers, in differentiating and assimilating those truths, and in reflecting and meditating on them in the recesses of his heart; while another beginner is engaged in sacrifice and in worship with "a leaf, a flower, a fruit, a handful of water";—a contrast indeed. Follow them a little further in their journey onwards, and you will find that sacrifice and worship are as much enjoined on the former as knowledge on the latter. To the former the teacher addresses as follows: "Be not inattentive to duties towards the Gods and the *pitṛs*. Regard thy mother as a God. Regard thy itinerant visitor as a God. Acts that are blameless; those should be performed; not others. What are our good examples; those should be followed by thee; not others." (*Taittirīya Upaniṣad*, XI.2). A spirit of devotion and worship is an essential condition for the knowledge of Brahman; and the more one knows Brahman, the more devoted and worshipful one becomes. And thus the 'gnostic' disappears in the devotee. Baladeva in the introduction to his commentary on the *Gītā* rightly observes: "It is knowledge that, with a certain qualification, is devotion. The indifference is like that of seeing without winking and seeing by a darting of the eye." The meaning is that knowledge of Brahman, becoming steady, is devotion. This point has been clared up by Rāmānuja in his Commentary on the *Vedāntasūtras*. "We admit," he there says, "that release consists only in the cessation of Nescience, and that this cessation results from the knowledge of Brahman. But a distinction has here to be made regarding the nature of this knowledge which the Vedānta texts aim at enjoining for the purpose of putting an end to Nescience. It is merely the knowledge of the sense of sentences which originates from the sentence? or is it knowledge in the form of meditation *(upāsanā)* which has the knowledge just referred to as its antecedent? Hence we conclude that the knowledge which the Vedānta texts aim at including is a knowledge of the sense of sentences, and denoted by *dhyāna*, *upāsanā* (i.e., meditation), and similar terms. 'Meditation' means steady remembrance, i.e., continuity of steady remembrance uninterrupted like the flow of oil; in agreement with the scriptural passage which declares steady remembrance to be the means of release: "On the attainment of remembrance all the ties are loosened" (*Ch. Up*., VII.xvi.2). (Thibaut's translation.) It is therefore the ignorance of the link between Knowledge and Devotion that is responsible for the popular misconception of the relation between them.

Now to return to our text. The One Hundred Aphorisms of Śāṇḍilya does not profess to teach an original doctrine of Devotion. It is a Mīmāṃsā of *bhakti,* that is, a compilation and exposition of illustrative authoritative texts on the main points in the doctrine of Devotion. To explain the nature of Mīmāṃsāśāstra, we give two examples below. (1) The *Chāndogya Upaniṣad*, II.xxiii.1, declares: "He who is steady in Brahman, attains immortality." The doubt arises whether 'steadiness' here means knowledge or devotion. The text discusses the point and concludes that 'steadiness' means devotion, and not knowledge. (2) The *Gītā*, IV.9, declares: "My birth and My action divine." Here the doubt arises as to the meaning of the word 'divine'. Some say that it means 'produced through merit'; others think that it means 'produced in heaven'. The text by implication rejects these interpretations, and explains that the word 'divine' means 'constituted by His own *māyā* only'. It would be wrong to suppose in these two cases, for instance, that the text declares immortality to be the fruit of Devotion and attributes divineness to the body of the Lord, and then supports its teachings by means of revealed texts. This character of the work should be always borne in mind.

The work is divided into three chapters containing two lectures each.

Incidentally it explains Creation and Dissolution, the causes of *saṃsāra* and *mukti*, the nature and function of the *ātman* and *manas*, the relation of the world, the *jīva*, and Brahman, and sources and objects of knowledge.

A complete outline of the work will be found in the elaborate table of contents which follows.

We beg however to invite special attention to the following teachings—

a. The cause of *saṃsāra* is want of Devotion and not want of knowledge of Brahman.

b. Like the foulness of the crystal in the presence of a China rose *saṃsāra* is foreign to the nature of the *jīva*, being merely a reflection from the mind.

c. The end of Devotion is not *mukti* but the pleasure of the Lord.

a. *Cause of saṃsāra:* The distinction drawn here between Devotion and knowledge is more popular than philosophical. Knowledge and Devotion have one and the same end in view, namely the removal of the circumstances which in the phenomenal world creates the division of the *jīva* and Brahman. Between them there is only a difference of degree and not of kind. Both elevate the mind to the highest state of purity; when the veil of the mind becomes so thin that the light of Brahman pierces through it, and the *jīva* is drawn, as it were, by an intense love, of kin to kin, towards Brahman. The mind is then immediately dissolved; and "nothing manifold is here". It is in this view of *mukti* resulting immediately through Devotion that the cause of *saṃsāra* is want of Devotion and not want of knowledge of Brahman. For, otherwise, in the lower stages of evolution towards *mukti* want of knowledge of Brahman inasmuch as the cause of the prolongation of *saṃsāra* as is want of Devotion.

b. *Nature of saṃsāra:* Take for example an eclipse of the sun. The moon comes in between the earth and the sun and causes the eclipse. The ignorant may imagine that somehow or other the light of the sun is extinguished and darkness envelops the universe. But they are wrong. Similarly, the mind intervenes and shuts off the light of Brahman from the *jīva*. Those who do not know the truth ever grope in darkness, without making any effort to remove the obstruction. This is the condition of the average man. He is a *saṃsārī* should he think, or should others who can distinguish the mind from the embodied *ātman* think, that this is their permanent state or that this state is connate with the nature of the *ātman*, they are under a grave error. *Saṃsāra* is no more natural to the *ātman* than darkness is to the sun. *Saṃsāra* is a temporary eclipse of the light of Brahman, which is not to be mistaken for a permanent state appertaining to the nature of the embodied *ātman*.

c. *End of devotion: Mukti* consists in the removal of the foulness reflected in the *ātman* from the mirror of the mind. This removal is possible only by the abolition of the mind through intense Devotion. It does not denote the accomplishment of something which did not exist before. It means merely the development of the bliss aspect of the *ātman* which in the *saṃsārī jīva* is manifested only in the aspects of existence and consciousness. The development of bliss in the gift of Brahman; and does not come to every devotee as a matter of course. So is it declared in the *Kaṭha Upaniṣad*, I.ii.23:

> "Not is this *ātman* by explanation to be gained, nor by intelligence, not by much learning;
> Whom alone it elects, by him it is to be gained; to him this *ātman* unfolds its own nature."

and also in ibidem, I.ii.20:

> "Subtler than the subtlest, greater than the greatest the *ātman* is hidden in the cavity of this *jīva*.
> Him the firm of faith in Viṣṇu sees, free from grief, through the grace of the Creator; (he sees also) the superiority (of the Lord) over himself."

On the other hand, a true devotee does not crave for *mukti*. He finds infinite joy in the service of the Lord. Thus, declares the *Bhāgavata*, III.xxv.34:

> "Not unity of self with Me desire some engaged in serving My feet, and doing acts for My sake,
> Those Bhāgavatas who, associating among themselves, extol My mighty deeds."

and again (III.xix.13):

> "Residence in the same world with me, lordliness equal to Mine, nearness to me, possession of My form, unity with me,
> Even if offered, they do not accept, save the privilege of doing service unto me."
> So dear the path of *bhakti*, says Jñāneśvara, "they despise the great Release."

The end of devotion then is not *mukti*, but the pleasure of the Lord.

And this Love of Devotion is reciprocated by Him. This is revealed in the *Ṛgveda*, IV.i.10, 55.

> "He alone in the secret by the humble in spirit is praised
> His beautiful mind, to the people, desirous to speak,
> The Giver of Blessings the source of joy becomes to the adorer, when

the Giver of Blessings, the Lord of Wealth, pervades the speech by His power."

"This salutation to the Giver of Blessings, the self-
Resplendent, the Eternal Power, for strength is offered.
May we, O God, in this battlefield (of the world), become all-round
victors along with the wise, being blessed by Thee."

"Holding my hand Thou leadest me,
My comrade everywhere;
As I go on and lean on Thee,
My burden Thou dost bear.
If as I go in my distress
I frantic words should say,
Thou settest right my foolishness,
And tak'st my shame away.
Thus Thou to me new hope dost send,
A new world bringest in,
Now know I every man a friend,
And all I meet my kin.
So like a happy child I paly
In Thy dear world, O God,
And everywhere,—I, Tuka, say,
Thy bliss is spread abroad."—Tukārāma

Introduction

THE LORD'S WILL BE DONE!

A commentary on the One Hundred Aphorisms of Śāṇḍilya is now expounded by the learned Svapneśvara, relying upon the Supreme Deity.

Great is the marvel of the honey of the two (lotus) feet of Govinda: which whoso drink are not bewildered, those who drink not are bewildered!

It will be declared (hereafter, cf. introduction to aphorism 93) that *mukti* is the *jīva*'s attaining Brahma-hood. (*Mukti* means release from the association of the body and absolute relief from the experience of pleasure and pain. The *jīvas* are the embodied souls. Brahma-hood is the state of Brahman, that is, the state of pure existence, pure intelligence, and pure bliss.) The *jīvas*, again, are in the end non-different from Brahman. Their *saṃsāra* (or succession of embodied existences) therefore, is not connate (with their nature). It is caused by the external influence of the internal organ (cf. mind). The internal organ is constituted by the three primary modifications of the primordial matter, called *sattva*, the luminous, *rajas*, the active, and *tamas*, the passive. The *jīva*'s *saṃsāra* is produced just in the same way as in the case of the crystal and the like redness and the like are produced through the propinquity of a China rose and the like.

And this (*saṃsāra*), for the very reason that it is externally caused, is not capable of being removed by Knowledge (which according to some is the means of *mukti*); for not even by the most skilful observation there is the cessation of the (optical) illusion of redness in the crystal, so long as there is the conjunction of the China rose. But it can be removed by the destruction either of the soul embodied in the *jīva* or of the internal organ, or else by the destruction of the connection between them.

Now, in the present case, the destruction of the soul embodied in the *jīva* is not possible, as the manifestation of all being depends on its existence. Nor is the destruction of its connection (with the internal organ) possible, as it is of their very essence that they should be connected (so long as the internal organ subsists). Reasoning by exhaustion, therefore, the cessation of the error (viz. that *saṃsāra* is an attribute of the soul) can take place only from the destruction of the proximate object or adjunct (i.e. the internal organ), and not from the knowledge of the soul.

And for the destruction of the internal organ another cause (than the one expounded by the advocates of Knowledge) is to be sought. And that cause is nothing else than Devotion to the Lord. Not being an object of perception or of reasoning, it is established by the Śrutis (Revelations) and the Smṛtis (Recollections). Thus, for instance, the *Bhagavadgītā* contains the passages which the Lord opens with the words—

"Of these, *sattva*, by reason of its being free from dirt, is illuminating and healthful;
It binds, O sinless, by attachment to pleasure and by attachment to knowledge.
Know *rajas* to be of the nature of passion, and arising out of attachment and thirst,
That binds the embodied soul, O son of Kuntī, by attachment to activity,
And know *tamas* to be the product of ignorance, and the cause of illusion to all embodied ones;
That binds, O Bharata, with carelessness, indolence and sleep."
(*Gītā*, XIV.6-8)

and which He winds up with the words—

"And whoso serves Me with the attachment of unwavering devotion,
He, having passed all these *guṇas* (modifications of primal Matter), becomes fit for realising Brahman." (Ibid., XIV.26)

In this passage the Lord himself declares that devotion to Him becomes the cause of *mukti* in the form of the attainment of the bliss of Brahman, through the dissolution of the internal organs constituted by the three primary modifications of the primordial Matter.

It does not follow that knowledge of the Self is useless; as it contributes to (the development of) devotion by washing away the impurity of unbelief. But the text proves that Knowledge is not competent to expel the influence of the reflection of the adjunct in the shape of the internal organ proximate (to the embodied soul). And so the same sense is manifest in such texts as—

"Whoso realises the Self beyond the *guṇas*, he attains to My state."
(*Gītā*, XIV.19)

"(Acts do not bind one) whose doubts have been cut away by knowledge." (Ibid., IV.41)

Nor is ignorance the cause of *saṃsāra*, so that it might be possible to assert that the cessation of *saṃsāra* takes place through knowledge, because there is no proof that this is so; and also because, in the absence of the cause, e.g. particles of silver, it is impossible that silver should arise from a shell mistaken for it. Moreover, the Śruti, "How, O gentle youth, could it thus be that Being should be produced from Non-being" (*Chāndogya Upaniṣad,* VI.ii.2), which brings out the existence of the cause by means of the existence of the effect, declares that the world indeed is real. *A fortiori* is the reality of the Supreme Lord's creation established by such Śrutis as "Whose will is true" (ibid., III.xiv.2). Neither has the great Bādarāyaṇa declared in any *sūtra* that the world was constituted by Ignorance; on the contrary, by refuting (the reality of) dream creation, he has established the reality of the waking world. Nor was this refutation meant to serve as in illustration, for there is no reason for making such an assumption.

On the other hand, it has not been proved that the properties of pleasure, etc., are connate to the soul. Pleasure and the like are not directly modifications of the soul. They are merely reflected in or attributed to the soul, just as are the qualities of fairness of complexion and the like (as when a man says 'I am fair', meaning that it is body that is fair). (They do not therefore prove the existence of the soul.) The perception of pleasure, etc., being an act or a change, must have an instrumental cause; in this inference, it is proper to hold, for the sake of simplicity, that producibility through an instrument is by means of co-inherence only, just as is the producibility of sound through the auricular organ (i.e., 'that portion of the indivisible ether walled off within the fleshly 'ear', in which sound inheres by intimate relation'). Others maintain that pleasure and the like inhere in the instrumental cause by intimate relation, because they are properties apprehensible by an organ which is without a beginning (i.e., the internal organ), just as is the case with sound (which is apprehensible by a portion of uncreated ether). On either view (producibility through the instrument is by means of co-inherence only), because (pleasure, etc., on the one hand, and sound, on the other, are) properties apprehensible by an organ which is devoid of touch. But the existence of the soul is proved from its being the cause of the manifestation of all being (for in the absence of a knower, nothing could be known). All this will become clear in the second lecture of the third chapter.

Therefore, from a desire to know the established truths on the subject of Devotion,—as in the case of Duty (in the Pūrvamīmāṃsā)—inasmuch as it is the cause of the attainment of man's highest end, proceeds the following aphorism.

CHAPTER I

The Nature of Devotion

LECTURE I: The Definition of Devotion

अथातो भक्तिजिज्ञासा ।।१।१।१।।

अथ (*atha*), now. अत: (*ataḥ*), therefore. भक्तिजिज्ञासा (*bhakti-jijñāsā*), desire to know devotion.

1. Now, therefore, (there is) a wish to know Devotion.—1

The word 'now' introduces the subject, and has not the sense of *sequence*; for it is not necessary that the practice of devotion should be commenced after a preliminary study of the Veda, because, as will be declared hereafter (vide aphorism 78), even the low born are entitled to the practice of Devotion. Nor does the word 'now' bear the sense of sequence to the previous attainment of the resources of self-restraint, etc.; because mere desire for *mukti* entitles any one to enter upon the path of Devotion. And so there is the *mantra*:

"Who at the beginning created Brahmā,
And who breathed forth the Vedas to him,
To Him, the Shining One, who reveals the Self and the Intellect,
Do I, desirous of *mukti*, fly for refuge."

(*Śvetāśvatara Upaniṣad*, VI.18)

Nor, again, has the word 'now' the sense of benediction (usual at the commencement of new work for its successful completion); as its mere utterance (quite apart from its sense) serves the purpose of a benediction. So then the meaning of the aphorism is that a discussion of the nature of Devotion ought to be undertaken by one who desires *mukti*. 'Discussion' is implied by the phrase 'a wish to know'.

Although Devotion in the form of attachment to the Supreme Lord is not like the Duty and its consequent Merit (of the Pūrvamīmāṃsā) something to be accomplished by action, nor is like the Brahman (of the Vedānta) something capable of being known; yet even when devotion has been perfected by its own cause, viz., merits acquired by one in previous lives, and secondary forms of devotion practised in the present life, its destruction is still possible by means of such false arguments as that "this is not devotion", "the highest good is not its end", "its object is not laudable", just as a wife's faith in her husband (is likely to be shaken by unfounded calumnies). It is by way of the refutation of these false objections that a discussion contributes to the culture of devotion. This is declared by the word 'therefore': Because the refutation of false objections is to be looked for, *therefore* is there a wish to know the nature of devotion. Hence there is the prayer for the unbroken flow of devotion in:

"In whatever thousands of births I may have to move, O Lord,
Through them all may my devotion, O Acyuta (Unchanging), remains constantly fixed on Thee." (*Viṣṇu Purāṇa,* I.xx.16)

Because such a prayer is needed (for the refutation of false arguments). For the same reason the accessories of devotion are also fruitful; a discussion is indeed fruitful.—1

Now devotion cannot enter into our understanding so long as it does not possess an intelligible form; and so long as it does not enter into our understanding, it cannot be made the subject of discussion. Hence its definition is (next) stated.

सा परानुरक्तिरीश्वरे ।। १ । १ । २ ।।

सा (*sā*), it. परा (*parā*), supreme, higher, primary. अनुरक्तिः (*anuraktiḥ*), attachment, affection, love. ईश्वरे (*īśvare*), in the Lord.

2. The higher Devotion is (absolute) attachment to the Lord.—2

In this aphorism, the words 'higher devotion' indicate the subject to be defined; the rest is the definition. The word 'higher' excludes the secondary or lower forms of devotion. The words 'to the Lord' contain the general import of the definition; devotion is simply of the nature of an affection which has for its object one who is worthy of being worshipped. But here for the purposes of our definition, devotion is nothing but a particular function of the internal organ regarding the Supreme Lord as its object, and its distinctive character is easily found by reference to worldly attachment, etc. As has been said by Prahlāda who possessed this higher devotion:

"May that undecaying satisfaction which the unreflecting feel in respect of worldly objects,
Never depart from my heart while I am ever remembering Thee."
(*Viṣṇu Purāṇa*, I.xx.17)

In this verse by the word 'satisfaction' it is affection inseparably associated with pleasure, that is implied. Otherwise, as satisfaction in the form of pleasure, (being a feeling merely), cannot have any object, the locative inflexion denoting object (in 'in respect of worldly objects') would be inappropriate; because, although it appears as the cognition of pleasure, since pleasure is the object of that cognition, it is impossible that 'worldly objects' should be the object of pleasure. Therefore, it is attachment or affection together with its proper object that is implied. Nor can 'satisfaction' mean pleasure produced by 'worldly objects', for there is no rule of grammar for the use of the locative inflecion to denote the producer or the originator. Moreover, in the passage "may my devotion, O Acyuta, remain constantly fixed on Thee" (*Viṣṇu Purāṇa,* I.xx.16), it is established that devotion has the Lord for its object; by the word 'satisfaction' (ibid., I.xx.17) also the same (devotion) is referred to; since the two verses convey the same sense. The distinction between the two verses is that in the first there is the prayer for devotion in each successive birth, while in the second there is the prayer, by the example of affection for worldly objects, that the same devotion might by all means be preserved. The idea of affection or attachment is necessary; because even satisfaction produced by worldly objects is not possible without affection or attachment. And so we have the aphorism of Patañjali:

"Attachment of affection is the running after pleasure."

(*Yogasūtram*, II.7)

It is this affection or attachment to which the character of devotion must belong, because it accompanies all the marks of devotion to be mentioned hereafter and also because this is the simplest explanation.

The character of Devotion does not belong to an occasional remembrance of the Lord nor to occasional hymns, etc., because they do not always go together. Neither does the character of Devotion belong to the mere knowledge about the Lord, because such knowledge is possible even in the case of those who had aversion, etc., towards Him. Nor even is Devotion the knowledge of the Lord as an object of worship, because Devotion is not invariably found present in all such acts of worship as adoration and bowing; and moreover, if it were so, then, even in regard to one who under the force of circumstances or through fear got the idea that bowing, etc., are to be done to the Lord, one would have to use such expressions as "he is a devotee", "he is attached to the Lord". If it is suggested that Devotion should be defined as the knowledge of the Lord as the object which is to be worshipped with affection, etc., let us rather say that it is affection or attachment that is Devotion. And so:

"Having their minds fixed upon Me, and their life directed to Me, enlightening one another,
And constantly talking about Me, (My devotees) become satisfied and delighted.
To these who are ever attached to Me and worship Me with affection,
I give that concentration of mind by which they attain to Me."

(*Gītā,* X.9-10)

in such texts the worship of those whose life and mind, etc., are devoted to Him, has been described, and not only of those who know Him as the object of worship. Hence also it is recollected (cf. *Viṣṇu Purāṇa,* V.xiii.22) that even the young milkmaids whose affection was excited by the sight of the lovely form of Kṛṣṇa, obtained *mukti* as the fruit of their devotion.

The prefix *anu* (in *anurakti*, affection), however, is not a part of the definition. But devotion has been defined as *anurakti* (*anu*, after, and *rakti*, affection), because it is produced *anu*, after, the knowledge of the greatness, etc., of the Almighty Lord.

You may ask: "If this were so, would it not follow that the characteristic of devotion proper belongs also to the affection which has the father, etc., as its objects, seeing that the whole world is pervaded by the Supreme Lord? If the reply is that the characteristic of devotion proper is to be predicated only in regard to a person who undergoes no change, then again, the definition would be too narrow and would not apply to the devotion of such persons as the milkmaids towards the Lord in His finite incarnations." To this we reply that Devotion is only that affection which has for its object a conscious being unconditioned by the adjunct of the *jīva*, i.e., the internal organ. Thus devotion towards an object conditioned by incarnation and devotion towards the All Full will be equally included.—2

तत्संस्थस्यामृतत्वोपदेशात् ।। १।१।३।।

तत्संस्थस्य (*tat-saṃstha-sya*), whose devotion is towards Him. अमृतत्वोपदेशात् (*amṛta-tva-upadeśāt*), from the teaching of immortality.

3. (An enquiry into the nature of devotion should not be abandoned, on the supposition that devotion is fruitless or produces minor results only), because there is the declaration that he who is devoted to the Lord, becomes immortal.—3

Tat-saṃstha is he who has *saṃsthā*, i.e., devotion, to *tat*, i.e., the Lord. In his case, immortality has been declared as the fruit (in the *Chāndogya Upaniṣad*, II.xxiii.1): "He who is steady in Brahman, attains immortality."

Therefore any possible indifference towards the enquiry on the ground of its being fruitless or bearing only inferior fruits, becomes avoided.—3

ज्ञानमिति चेन्न द्विषतोऽपि ज्ञानस्य तदसंस्थितेः ।।१।१।४।।

ज्ञानम् (*jñānam*), knowledge. इति (*iti*), so. चेत् (*cet*), if. न (*na*), no. द्विषतः (*dviṣataḥ*), of the hater, of the antagonist. अपि (*api*), also. ज्ञानस्य (*jñānasya*), of knowledge. तदसंस्थितेः (*tat-a-saṃsthiteḥ*), not being steadiness in Him.

4. (If you say 'steadiness in Brahman' means) knowledge (of Brahman, we reply) no, because the knowledge (of Brahman) possessed by one who hates Him, is not (spoken of as) steadiness in Him.—4

If you say that "by the words 'steadiness in Brahman' knowledge of Brahman it is that is meant, and not devotion to Him; so that the fruit of immortality belongs to him only who knows Him", (we reply that) there is no such flaw (in our interpretation of the text). 'Steadiness' is nothing but devotion; it is not knowledge, because one who hates an object is not spoken of as being 'steady' in that object, even though he may know all about it. Thus, for instance, the ministers, friends, etc., who are attached to a king, etc., are spoken of as being steady in him, but not also his rival kings. For, the determination of the sense of a word must be made in the case of Vedic literature also in the very same way as it is made in the case of secular literature. And so, in the story of Cirakārika, transgression of devotion towards the husband has been described in the verse:

"During that time having reflected on that failure of *saṃsthā* in his wife,
The sage spoke thus distressed, shedding tears in his sorrow." (Cowell)
(*Mahābhārata,* Śānti Parva, CCLXVII.6526)

It follows therefore that *saṃsthā* or steadiness as used in the *Chāndogya* text means devotion. And similarly the very same meaning is to be concluded also in the case of the aphorism of Bādarāyaṇa.

"(The Creator of the universe is *Nirguṇa* Brahman and not *Saguṇa*), because the devoted to Him attains salvation, according to the teaching (of the scriptures)."—*Vedāntasūtram,* I.i.7.—4

तयोपक्षयाच्च ।।१।१।५।।

तया (*tayā*), by it, i.e., devotion. उपक्षयात् (*upakṣayāt*), because of inferiority. च (*ca*), and also.

5. ('Steadiness' does not mean knowledge), also because *knowl-*

***edge* pales into insignificance before Devotion (as a means of *mukti*).—5**

Because in regard to *mukti*, Knowledge is rendered pale by it, i.e., devotion. The phrase 'and also' is intended to show that the argument now put forward should be taken along with the one given before.

Cf. such texts as:

"Those who offer sacrifices unto the Gods, go to the Gods; My devotees likewise go to Me." (*Gītā*, VII.23)

Cf. also the words of the Lord addressed to Prahlāda:

"As thy mind filled with faith in me wavers not.
So thou, by my favour, shalt even go to *nirvāṇa*."
(Cowell, *Viṣṇu Purāṇa*, I.xx.20)

So much is established.

You may say that in the text "Only by knowing Him one goes beyond death; there is no other path for going" (*Śvetāśvatara Upaniṣad*, III.8), it is heard that *mukti* is the fruit of knowing, and that if the Smṛtis appear to contradict this revelation, they must be given a different interpretation. We reply that such is not the case. Here also devotion it is that supersedes knowledge. For thus the word *ati-mṛtyu*, beyond-death, is not a conventional synonym of *mukti*, but is a derivative conventionally used in the sense of *mukti* according to its derivation (in the *upapada* sense) that it is that which being present the passing beyond death takes place. Preferably to this derivation, let devotion itself be denoted by the word *ati-mṛtyu* derived (as a 'case') as that, i.e., devotion, by means of which the passing beyond death takes place; in accordance with the rule of grammar that the sense of the case-affix is of superior force to the sense of the *upapada* affix (cf. Pāṇini, II.iii.19); because the passing beyond death through devotion is obtained from such texts as:

"To those, O prince, whose hearts are fixed on me,
I shall ere long be the deliverer from the sea of the world and death."
(Cowell, *Gītā*, XII.7)

There is also the *mantra:*

"We worship the three-eyed, of sweet fragrance, the giver of nourishment;
Like the cucumber from its stem, may we be released from mortality, but not from immortality." (*Ṛgveda*, V.vii.59.12)

Here 'worship' means devotion, since the *kalpa* of this *mantra* explains it in the very same sense. Nor can it be said that devotion is too far from this Śruti (where the word has not been used at all), for the same objection would equally apply to *mukti* also. Therefore from the everlasting Śruti it is the supersession of knowledge (by devotion) that is perceived.—5

"But still", it may be asked, "what is the reason for supposing that devotion has the form of affection?" There being room for such an enquiry, the author declares:

द्वेषप्रतिपक्षभावाद्रसशब्दाच्च रागः ।।१।१।६।।

द्वेषप्रतिपक्षभावात् (*dveṣa-pratipakṣa-bhāvāt*), because of its being the opposite of hatred. रसशब्दात् (*rasa-śabdāt*), from the word *rasa,* sweetness. च (*ca*), and. रागः (*rāgaḥ*), affection, attachment.

6. (Devotion is affection), because it is the opposite of hatred, and from the use of the word *rasa* (in the Veda in reference to devotion).—6

Devotion deserves to be an affection and nothing else; why? because it is the opposite of hatred. For, in secular language, the expressions "he is a hater", "he is devoted" are used in reference to persons possessing the two mutually contradictory attributes; and amongst men it is affection and not knowledge, etc., that is universally known to be the opposite of hatred. Likewise in the *Viṣṇu Purāṇa,* having first mentioned Śiśupāla's persistent hatred towards the Lord, it is said:

"This Lord, if named or called to recollection even in the relation of hatred, grants a fruit which is hard to be obtained by all the gods and demons; what will he not grant to those who possess perfect devotion?"

(*Viṣṇu Purāṇa,* IV.xv.12)

So again in the Smṛti of Atri, it is said:

"Remembering Govinda even through hatred, Śiśupāla, the son of Damaghoṣa, went to heaven; what to say of one who is wholly dependent upon Him?"

Here too devotion has been represented as being the opposite of hatred. Similarly also in the *Gītā:*

"Those detractors who hate me (present) in their own and others' bodies,
Those fierce haters, the vilest of men in their mortal lives,
I continually throw, wicked as they are, into the wombs of demon

mothers.
Born in a demon womb, deluded from birth to birth,
And never finding me, O son of Kuntī, they go thence the lowest road."
(Cowell, *Gītā,* XVI.18-20)

And, as the opposite of this hatred, it is proper that devotion should be described as that affection only which has the Lord for its object.

Moreover, from the revelation, "having obtained the *rasa,* sweetness, he became full of bliss" (*Taittirīya Upaniṣad,* II.vii.1), it is known that *rasa* which has Brahman as its object, is the cause of *mukti* which is the manifestation of the bliss of Brahman. And that *rasa* is affection is well-known in such texts as:

"(Objects withdraw from him who withdraws his senses, but) *rasa* or affection or attachment remains; having seen the Supreme, the self-centred man's *rasa* or attachment also retires." (*Gītā,* II.59)

Here *rasa* means affection for worldly objects. Hence also, after describing the ascent of Rāma, Lakṣmaṇa, and others to the heavenly world, the word *anurāga,* affection, has been directly applied to devotion in the passage.

"Whose of the residents of the city of Kosala had affection for those partial manifestations of the Lord, they too, having their minds absorbed in them, attained the status of residing together with them in the same world." (*Viṣnu Purāṇa*, IV.iv.4)

From this also it follows that it is not knowledge, but devotion in the form of affection, that has the highest good as its fruit.

It may be contended that, that devotion is the opposite of hatred is not necessarily the mark of its being affection, because it may as well be the mark of a neutral state of mind, and the reasoning will then be inconclusive. To this it is replied that the result of hatred is cessation of activity, while the opposite of it is activity. And activity does take place on the part of those who are devoted in the faithful service, etc., rendered to the adorable object, while there is cessation of activity on the part of those who have the opposite feeling in such service, etc. So also the statement that devotion is the opposite of hatred is made (in the aphorism) with reference to the opposition between them by way of their respective effects. Thus the construction of the argument is as follows—

Devotion must be of the form of affection which has the adorable one as its object,

Because it is a particular attribute of the soul which is different from the knowledge that it is the means for the accomplishment of any particular good and which is the incentive to faithful service to the adorable one;

Whatever is not so, is not so,
As for example, is hatred.

There is also another argument in support of the definition, namely that along with the increase of affection a corresponding increase is seen to take place in the faithful service, etc., rendered to the object of worship. Moreover, it is commonly known that whoever is devoted to a certain object there is in him the absence of indifference towards that object. This being so, devotion must be of the form of that attribute which is the opposite of hatred and which is helpful to such faithful service, etc.; because it is a particular attribute of the soul which is the incentive to service; as, for example, is the knowledge that a certain thing is the means for the accomplishment of a particular good. Next, together with the elimination of the characteristic of its being the knowledge that it is the means for the accomplishment of a particular good, it is proved by reasoning from exhaustion that devotion has the nature of affection. And again the argument *a fortiori* "what will he not grant to those who possess perfect devotion?" contained in the above passage of the *Viṣṇu Purāṇa,* and also in such texts as "For they too who may be of mean births, by taking refuge in Me, reach the highest state. . . . What to say of pious Brāhmaṇas" (*Gītā,* IX.32-33), should be understood to have reference only to the opposite of hatred. As hatred is the cause of *saṃsāra* according to the text 'Me in their own and in others' bodies . . .' (*Gītā,* XVI.18), so its opposite attribute is nothing but the affection which has the Supreme Self as its object unassociated with the adjunct of the *jīva,* i.e. the internal organ. It is this affection which in the form of devotion becomes the cause of the destruction of *saṃsāra.* The same idea is contained in the text "Never finding Me. . . ." (*Gītā,* XVI.20)

From the expression 'and also' in the aphorism, it is inferred that devotion is an affection, because it develops the marks of affection such as horripilation, etc. For such marks are well-known in such passages as "She reveals her affection for me by her cheek with its down erect" (*Śakuntalā,* Act III). On the other hand, were devotion not an affection but a different feeling, there would be the fault of redundancy in the supposition that these identical marks were the characteristics of a different thing.

And this affection, according to some (i.e., the Mīmāṃsakas), is merely a form of volition, as it also arises from the knowledge that it is the means for the accomplishment of a desired end, as is the case in sacrifice, etc. But we hold that affection is quite distinct from volition, as is hatred, because the intuitions of affection are in the form of "I am pleased", "I am affected", and not in the form of "I will". Moreover, volition is directed only to an end which has not been accomplished, while objects both accomplished and unaccomplished are equally the objects of affection. In fact, to be brief, the supposition that this affection pervades the characteristic mark of volition, etc., will be vitiated by the fault of redundancy.

Therefore, our definition of devotion is not shaken.—6

It may be apprehended that devotion is essentially an action, and that an action is not competent to produce the highest good, according to such revelations as "not by action, nor by progeny, nor by wealth, but by renunciation, have some attained to immortality" (*Taittirīya Āraṇyaka*, X.x.21). To refute this apprehension the author declares:

न क्रिया कृत्यनपेक्षणाज्ज्ञानवत् ।। १ । १ । ७ ।।

न (*na*), not. क्रिया (*kriyā*), action. कृत्यनपेक्षणात् (*kṛti-an-apekṣaṇāt*), because of not requiring an effort of will. ज्ञानवत् (*jñāna-vat*), like knowledge.

7. (Devotion is) not an action, because, like knowledge, it does not follow an effort of will.—7

This devotion does not deserve to be essentially an action, because it does not result from an effort of will. Whatever is not consequent on an effort of will, is not essentially an action, as for example knowledge.* For knowledge is dependent upon the presence of evidence, and a man cannot, by an effort of will, produce it, or not produce it, or make it otherwise. So too with devotion. For the affection felt by a man for wife, son, and the like, is not produced in its different manifestations by the man's own effort of will. But devotion is dependent for its production on such means as merits acquired in previous births, secondary forms of devotion, etc.—7

अत एव फलानन्त्यम् ।। १ । १ । ८ ।।

अतः (*ataḥ*), hence. एव (*eva*), indeed. फलानन्त्यम् (*phala-ānantyam*), endlessness of fruit.

8. Hence indeed is the endlessness of (its) fruit.—8

*There is an important technical *śloka* current among the Pandits, *Jñāna-janya bhavet icchā, icchā-janya bhavet kṛtiḥ, kṛti-janya bhavecceṣṭā, ceṣṭā-janya bhavet kriyā. Kṛti* here means *yatna*, 'volition'. "From knowledge arises desire, from desire volition from volition conscious exertion of the muscles, and from this action." (Cowell)

Since devotion is not essentially an action, therefore, it is established that fruit, i.e., the highest good, is endless. Otherwise, the non-permanence of even immortality would be entailed in accordance with the revelation: "Just as here the world gained by action perishes, so too hereafter the world gained by merit perishes." (*Chāndogya Upaniṣad*, VIII.i.6)—8

तद्वतः प्रपत्तिशब्दाच्च न ज्ञानमितरप्रपत्तिवत् ।। १।१।६।।

तद्वतः (*tat-vataḥ*), of one who has that, i.e., knowledge. प्रपत्तिशब्दात् (*prapatti-śabdāt*), from the revelation of worship. च (*ca*), also. न (*na*), not. ज्ञानम् (*jñānam*), knowledge. इतरप्रपत्तिवत् (*itara-prapatti-vat*), like the other revelations of worship.

9. And also from the revelation about worship by one who has knowledge, (Devotion is) not knowledge, as (there is no mention of knowledge in the revelations about) inferior worship.—9

For there is the word of the Lord:

"At the end of many births he who has knowledge worships Me.
One who realises that Vāsudeva is all, such a great soul is hard to be found." (*Gītā,* VII.19)

In this verse worship by one who has knowledge is mentioned. This would be inappropriate, were devotion to be the cause of knowledge, "as there is no mention of knowledge in the revelations about inferior worship." Thus immediately after the above declaration, the *Gītā* proceeds to say: "Having their knowledge robbed by such and such various desires, they worship inferior deities" (VII.20). Hereby it is by way of blaming the worship of other deities that worship is (indirectly) praised. In this verse it is the devotion to the deities, and not the knowledge of them, that is described by the word worship; for worship in the very same sense is that which one can recognise as used in both the verses.

From the word 'also' in the aphorism it is inferred that the mention of worship in close sequence to knowledge is yet another reason for devotion lacking the character of knowledge. For instance,

"Whosoever thus freed from delusion knows Me to be the Highest Person,
He knowing all, O Bhārata, worships Me in every way." (*Gītā,* XV.19)

And so again,

"(Great souls), having known Me as the origin of all being and immutable, worship Me with minds not fixed on anything else."
(Ibid., IX.13)

and again,

"Thus having known, the wise worship Me, filled with rapture."

(Ibid., X.8)

Therefore, devotion not essentially knowledge.

Although, by the mark of its being an affection, its difference from knowledge has been already established, the present aphorism is intended to dispel the apprehension that the word devotion means, in a secondary sense, the knowledge of Brahman.

This however has to be considered, namely that the words of the *Bhagavadgītā* are not authoritative in the form of a revelation as the Vedas are, but as being a Smṛti or recollection recorded in the *Mahābhārata;* and that this being so, how is the *Gītā* referred to in the aphorism by the expression "from the revelation?" Here some explain the reference as meaning, from the revelation which is inferred (as being the original of the recollection recorded in the *Gītā*). Here we say that what constitutes a Veda is the fact that it is an utterance of the Lord in reference to unseen objects, and that this characteristics is equally present in the *Gītā* texts. Hence is found the epigraph (at the end of each chapter of the *Gītā*): "Thus in the *Bhagavadgītā Upaniṣats.*" Those same 'revelations' have only been recorded in verse by Vyāsa. And so declares another Purāṇa:

"The *Gītā* is to be attentively recited, what need is there of other long compilations of *śāstras*?
That *Gītā,* which itself issued from the lotus-mouth of Padmanābha."

(Cowell, *Gītā*)

Nor is there in this view the implication that the Śūdras are not to hear the *Gītā* (like the Vedas, both being revelations); because by the general permission itself for all castes and all sexes to hear the *Mahābhārata,* the competence of the Śūdras to hear the *Gītā,* as also the praises of the sacred syllable, is established. It cannot be maintained that the permission to hear the *Mahābhārata* is subject to the exclusion of the *Gītā;* as without the *Gītā* the sum total of 100,000 verses which is the *Mahābhārata,* cannot be completed. And so has it been declared by the teachers:

"Those very *mantras* of the Vedas, inserted in the *Mahābhārata* and other works, they use in a secular sense, without observing the rules of Vedic study."—9

Thus ends the first lecture of the first chapter in the Commentary on the One Hundred Aphorisms of Śāṇḍilya composed by the most learned teacher Svapneśvara.

LECTURE II: The Accessories of Devotion

Thus Devotion having been defined as the invariable and unconditional antecedent of immortality, there is the commencement of the second lecture in order to discriminate Knowledge, Concentration (*yoga*) and Devotion in their relation of being respectively the accessory and the principal.

सा मुख्येतरापेक्षितत्वात् ।। १ । २ । १ ।।

सा (*sā*), it, devotion. मुख्या (*mukhyā*), principal. इतरापेक्षितत्वात् (*itara-apekṣita-tvāt*), being required, depended on, presupposed, implied by the others, i.e., knowledge, yoga, etc.

1. Devotion is the principal thing, because knowledge and yoga subserve it.—10

The reference, 'it', is for the recollection of what was stated at the close of the first lecture. 'It', the higher devotion or devotion proper, is 'principal', the main thing, because 'by the others,' i.e., by knowledge of soul, yoga, etc., it is regarded as that to which they are to make their own contribution. In the *Chāndogya Upaniṣad,* in the passage (VII.xiv.24) which opens with the words, "that which is immensity is bliss", it is revealed: "The Self is all this. He who sees thus, thinks thus, knows thus, gets affection for the Self, sports with the Self, is mated to the Self, rejoices in the Self; he becomes his own ruler." Here the 'seeing' alluded to in the phrase "who sees thus", becomes an accessory to the higher devotion in the form of affection for the Self, by way of the refutation of such errors as that it is not lovable, etc. Just an in such cases as "the ascetic bearing the staff repeats the initiatory phrase after the preceptor", "he causes the cow to be milked, wearing the sacred thread reversed", "knowing he offers sacrifice", "being wealthy he is happy", etc., the staff, etc., are the accessories, so too is 'seeing' an accessory to affection. 'Thinking' and 'knowing' have been recited because they logically come in as further establishing the point. Similarly, the expressions "sports with the Self", etc., are merely a repetition occasioned by the context, since sporting, etc., are invariable accompaniments of affection. Otherwise, if 'seeing', etc., were (intended to be) enjoined in reference to 'affection'; or if 'affection'; etc., were (intended to be) enjoined in reference to 'seeing', etc., the sentences would have been different (instead of having been combined into a single sentence as clauses). Therefore, 'seeing' is a subsidiary thing, according to the maxim: "A thing is called subsidiary, because it serves the end of another" (*Pūrvamīmāṃsā,* III.i.2). Hence the divine Manu also has declared that the affection for the Self is the principal thing in:

"The Muni who abandoning natural action, has constant affection for the Self,
Can realise his identity with the soul of all beings, he goes the highest road." (*Mahābhārata,* Śānti Parva, CLXLIV.7111-12)—1

प्रकरणाच्च ॥ १ । २ । २ ॥

प्रकरणात् (*prakaraṇāt*), from the topic under discussion, from the context. च (*ca*), also.

2. From the context also (it follows that 'seeing' is subsidiary to devotion).—11

The section (*Chāndogya Upaniṣad,* VII.24) deals with affection principally, because it is affection which bears the fruit (i.e., *mukti*). It is proper that 'seeing' appearing in the same section should be subsidiary.—2

दर्शनफलमिति चेन्न तेन व्यवधानात ॥ १ । २ । ३ ॥

दर्शनफलम् (*darśana-phalam*), fruit of seeing. इति (*iti*), thus. चेत् (*cet*), if. न (*na*), no. तेन (*tena*), by the pronoun, he. व्यवधानात् (*vyavadhānāt*), because of interception.

3. If (you say that immortality is) the fruit of 'seeing', (we reply), no, because of interception by (the pronoun) 'he'.—12

If you say that it is of the 'seeing' that immortality characterised as perpetual residence in the world of the Lord, is the fruit, so that the section will have 'seeing', and not affection, as the principal theme, and that thus the table will be turned againt us, we reply, No, because of interception by the pronoun, 'he'. By the word 'he' in "he becomes a dweller in the world of the Lord", it is the nearest subject, namely the one who "gets affection for the Self", that is brought forward, and not the remote subject 'he who sees thus', since there is no reason why the reference should be to that which is separated. If you say that the section itself would be such a reason; we reply, No, as that would entail the fallacy of reasoning in a circle.—3

दृष्टत्वाच्च ॥ १ । २ । ४ ॥

दृष्टत्वात् (*dṛṣṭa-tvāt*), from being seen. च (*ca*), also.

4. (That knowledge is a cause of affection, and not *vice versa,* follows) also from this being seen (to be so in ordinary life).—13

For it is seen in ordinary life that the knowledge of beauty, etc., becomes the cause of a young woman's affection for a young man, but not that affection becomes the cause of knowledge. The subsidiary character of knowledge is ascertained also from the fact that it is seen to subserve affection. Thus, it is seen that (at first) the knowledge that Nature is cruel, worthless, unlovely, etc., is the cause of impurity of mind to living beings, that then from the knowledge that the Self is all-merciful, of unlimited majesty, and of infinite beauty, takes place the removal of that impurity; and that thereafter arises the higher devotion. Hence it is recited:

"They who think of the Supreme, whose souls are bound up in Him, who abide in Him, and find their refuge in Him,
They go thither whence there is no return, having all their sins removed by knowledge" (Cowell, *Gītā,* V.17)

And so too in the *Āyurveda:*

"Thought, firmness, and knowledge of soul, etc., are the best medicine of the mind's ailings." (Cowell, *Aṣṭāṅgahṛdaya,* I.23)—4

अत एव तदभावाद्वल्लवीनाम् । १ । २ । ५ । ।

अतः (*ataḥ*), hence. एव (*eva*), verily. तदभावात् (*tat-abhāvāt*), from the absence of that, i.e., knowledge. वल्लवीनाम् (*vallavīnām*), of the milk-maids.

5. Hence indeed (there was *mukti*) of the milkmaids in the absence of knowledge (in them, because knowledge is merely a subsidiary).—14

Just because knowledge is an accessory seen to be subservient to another's end, hence, rejecting the familiar aid of knowledge, since impurity of mind, etc., had no place in them, it is recollected that *mukti* accrued to the milkmaids solely by means of devotion to the Lord, which is the principal means of *mukti.* For instance.

"Virtuous, having all her merits cancelled by the intense rapture of thinking about Him,
And all her sins expiated by the agony of not obtaining Him,
Meditating on Him, the cause of the world, identical with the supreme Brahman,
Ceasing to breathe, one damsel of the Gopas obtained liberation."
(*Viṣṇu Purāṇa,* V.xiii.22)

Here, by the mark of pleasure and pain, affection is inferred; whereby *mutki* was attained;—such is the meaning of the passage. Just as the production of the fruit (of the sacrifice) is (by means of the act performed) even with unshelled golden berries (without the exclusion of shells from the beginning); so, in the case of the milkmaids, *mukti* resulted from affection (without the preliminary operation of removing the foulness of mind by means of knowledge), since in them there was no foulness of mind at all. Hence also it is known that knowledge is nothing but a subsidiary means. If it were the principal means, there would be no fruit (i.e., *mukti*) in its absence. Nor can the 'thinking about Him' be the knowledge of the identity of the soul and Brahman, because there were not present at the same time the other causes of such knowledge, such as hearing, pondering, etc. (as laid down in the *Bṛhadāraṇyaka Upaniṣad,* IV.iv.5), but the thinking was nothing but remembrance kept up or made constant by affection. Nor is this an *arthavāda,* (i.e., an inducement to the observance of an injunction previously laid down); because *arthavādas* have merits as the objects they aim at, and also because there is no injunction near (for the observance of which an inducement might be needed).—5

भक्त्या जानातीति चेन्नाभिज्ञप्त्या साहाय्यात् ।। १ । २ । ६ ।।

भक्त्या (*bhaktyā*), by devotion. जानाति (*jānāti*), knows. इति (*iti*), thus. चेत् (*cet*), if. न (*na*), no. अभिज्ञप्त्या (*abhijñaptyā*), by the knowledge of the previously known, by recognition. साहाय्यात् (*sāhāyyāt*), from the support.

6. If (you contend that the expression, *Gītā,* XVIII.55) **"he knows (Me) by devotion" (proves that devotion is the cause of knowledge, and not that knowledge is the cause of devotion, as we hold), (we reply). No, relying on the support (lent to our view) by (the phrase) 'recognition'.—15**

The author now introduces a possible objection and solves it. The objection is that the arguments based on the "section" (aphorism 11), "position of the word" (aphorism 12), and "mark" (aphorism 14) are precluded, *because our view is (as suggested) in contradiction to the Śrutis. For instance, there is the Śruti,

*"The Mīmāṃsā arranges the proofs that one thing is ancillary to another in the following order. (1) Śruti or a definite text, as 'let him offer with curds' where curds are clearly an ancillary part of the sacrifice. (2) *Liṅga*, 'sign' or 'the sense of the words' as leading to an inference, as in the text 'he divides by the ladle'; here we infer that the thing divided must be a liquid like ghee, since a ladle could not divide solid things like the baked flour cakes. (3) *Vākya* 'the being mentioned in one sentence': as in the text (I cut) thee for food, thus saying, 'he cuts the branch'; here the words ('I cut) thee for food' are ancillary

"By devotion he (re)cognises Me, how great and what I am in My essence;

Then having known Me in My essence, he forthwith enters into Me."

(*Gītā,* XVIII.55)

In this text, just as in the text "he attends to the *gārhapatya* fire with an *aindrī* verse" (*Taittirīya Saṃhitā*, I.v.8) (the third case-ending in *aindryā* denotes that the *aindrī* verse is the instrument), so, by the Śruti employing the case-ending (in *bhaktyā,* by devotion) which (as mentioned before, under I.i.5) is of superior force, it is determined that devotion is the cause of knowledge. Although, by the aphorism (13) "(That knowledge is a cause of affection, and not *vice versa*, follows) also from its being seen (to be so in ordinary life)", no room is left for calling in the aid of the Śruti, since the observed subservience of knowledge to devotion is within the reach of sense-perception, still it is not within the reach of sense-perception that affection having Brahman for its object is (to be) subserved by knowledge of which the object is Brahman; but by the observation of the fact that this is so in the case of the affection of young girls, etc., the same is to be inferred also in the case of the affection which has Brahman as its object. So that the reasoning ends in the establishment of a "mark of inference" (which, as stated, is precluded by the contrary revelation under consideration).

We reply that there is no such defect in our argument. The defect would have been entailed, had the *Gītā* said only "he cognises"; but it is not so. It has said "he recognises". Recognition is said to be the cognition of that which had been previously cognised. Thus, previous cognition subserving devotion is the promoter of devotion appearing in the form of the fruit of

to the action of cutting. (4) *Prakaraṇa*, 'the subject-matter viewed as a whole with an interdependence of its parts 'as in the *darśa-pūraṇamāsa* sacrifice; where the *prayāja* ceremonies, which have no special fruit mentioned, produce, as parts, a mystic influence (*apūrva*) which helps forward that influence of the whole by which the worshippers obtain heaven. Here the *prakaraṇa* proves them to be ancillary. (5) *Sthāna* 'relative position' or 'order' as the recital of the hymn *sundadhvam,* etc., 'be ye purified for the divine work' in connection with the mention of the *sannayya* vessels, where this position proves that the hymn is ancillary to the action of the sprinkling those vessels. (6) *Samakhya*, 'title' thus *Yajurveda* is called the special book for the *adhvaryu* priests, hence in any rite mentioned in it they are *prima facie* to be considered as the priests employed. The order represents the relative weight attached to each, the first, Śruti, being the most important, the last, *samakhya,* the least. (Cf. Jaimini's *Sutras,* III.3.1-14: *Nyāyamālāvistāra,* III.3.1-11; *Mīmāṃsāparibhāṣā*, pp. 8, 9; *Vedāntasūtras,* III.3.44.49). The objector in the text maintains that (4), (5) and (2) are precluded here by the Śruti (1) from the *Bhagavadgīta.*"—(Cowell) devotion.* Thereafter, till it becomes firm, devotion requires the aid of knowledge in the form of recognition (i.e., constant remembrance), just as in the case of the shelling of rice which is continued by the shelling of separate grains (till the whole rice becomes clean). In order to point out that knowledge aids its effect (i.e., the effect of devotion), it is said: 'then', i.e., after devotion has been made firm by the firmness of knowledge, he "enters into Me". Therefore, this is not a Śruti, but a recital (*anuvāda*) which has logically come in.—6

The author makes the same sense clear (in the next aphorism).

प्रागुक्तं च ।। १ । २ । ७ ।।

प्राक् (*prāk*), before. उक्तं (*uktaṃ*), declared. च (*ca*), and.

7. And (this had been) declared before.—16

Before the passage "by devotion he re-cognises Me", after having stated "he becomes fit for realising Brahman" (*Gītā*, XVIII.53), it is declared:

> "Having become Brahman, being contented in soul, he grieves not, nor desires
> Feeling perfect equanimity towards all beings, he obtains the highest faith in me." (Cowell, *Gītā,* XVIII.54)

But as the devotee mentioned herein, as one who has already known Brahman, has no need of knowledge (of Brahman), it is but right that the following verse (*Gītā,* XVIII.55) should be taken to be a recital (*anuvāda,* and not the declaration of a new fact).—7

एतेन विकल्पोऽपि प्रत्युक्तः ।। १ । २ । ८ ।।

एतेन (*etena*), by this. विकल्पः (*vikalpaḥ*), alternative, interchangeable. अपि (*api*), also. प्रत्युक्तः (*pratyuktaḥ*), answered, refuted.

8. By this (the view that knowledge and devotion are) alternative (to each other as the means of *mukti*) is also refuted.—17

It should be considered that By this, i.e., by the ascertainment that knowledge is a subsidiary, the view also that here (i.e., as a means of *mukti*) knowledge and devotion are alternative to each other (i.e., both are equally efficient means of *mukti*), is 'answered', i.e., refuted. For the principal and the subsidiary cannot be mutually alternative in regard to one and the same

*Cf. *Nārada Bhaktisūtram,* aphorism 30, where it is declared that Devotion is the fruit of itself.

end. The word 'also' implies that the view that knowledge and devotion are conjoint means of *mukti* is also refuted on the same ground.—8

देवभक्तिरितरस्मिन् साहचर्य्यात् ।। १ । २ । ६ ।।

देवभक्तिः (*deva-bhaktiḥ*), devotion to a god. इतरस्मिन् (*itarasmin*), in another god. साहचर्य्यात् (*sāhacaryyāt*), because of being associated with.

9. The (expression) "devotion to a god" (refers) to another (than the Supreme), as it is coupled with (the expression "devotion to a spiritual teacher").—18

Sometimes it is heard from the Śruti:

"He who has supreme devotion to a god, and, as to a god, so to a spiritual teacher,
To him, verily great of soul, all these objects as declared reveal themselves." (*Śvetāśvatara Upaniṣad,* VI.23)

Here "devotion to a god" is to be understood to refer to a god other than the Lord; why? because it is associated with "devotion to a spiritual teacher"; for there can be no such association in the case of that devotion the fruit of which is immortality. But Indra and other gods, being worshipped, secure the fruit, knowledge, to the worshipper, as they do earthly good. Association (of one word with another word) also cause ascertainment; as in the case of the world *ulūka* (meaning an owl; Indra; the son of Śakuni, a warrior in the war of the Mahābhārata; Kaṇāda, etc., the reference of which in a given place is ascertained) through its association (with the other words of the context).

This explanation is added as confirmatory of the argument stated before (in aphorism 15).—9

योगस्तूभयार्थमपेक्षणात् प्रयाजवत् ।। १ । २ । १० ।।

योगः (*yogaḥ*), concentration, yoga. तु (*tu*), but, again. उभयार्थम् (*ubhaya-artham*), for the sake of both, i.e., knowledge and devotion. अपेक्षणात् (*apekṣaṇāt*), from being looked to, needed, depended on. प्रयाजवत् (*prayāja-vat*), like the ceremony of *prayāja*.

10. Yoga, however, is for the sake of both (knowledge and devotion), since both look to it (for aid); as is the case with the *prayāja* ceremony.—19

Yoga, again, is for the sake of knowledge and is also for the sake of devotion; since a concentrated state of mind is required by both.

If you ask that, in view of the maxim, "there is no connection between subsidiaries, as, being equally for the end of the principal, they stand on the same level" (*Pūrvamīmāṃsā,* III.i.22), how can yoga which is a subsidiary of the principal (i.e., devotion), be said to be a subsidiary of the subsidiary (i.e., knowledge)? The author replies "as is the case with the *prayāja* ceremony." As the *prayāja* ceremony is a subsidiary of the *vājapeya* and other sacrifices, and is also a subsidiary of the *dīkṣaṇīya* and other parts thereof, so it is here; since the identical reason exists in both the cases to make out the sense of a subsidiary having another subsidiary as its own subsidiary. Where, (however), the practice of yoga is undertaken for the sake of knowledge pure and simple, yoga does not subserve devotion.

In the same way dispassion towards worldly objects is to be considered as being for the benefit of both.—10

But you may say that it is hard to gainsay the recollection of Patañjali, "Or, through the contemplation of God" (*Yogasūtram,* I.23), where the worship of the Lord denoted by the word 'contemplation' is said to serve the end of producing *samādhi,* trance, and then you may ask "how then can devotion be the principal means?" To this the author replies:

गौण्या तु समाधिसिद्धिः ।। १ । २ । ११ ।।

गौण्या (*gauṇyā*), by the secondary, lower, (form of devotion). तु (*tu*), but. समाधिसिद्धिः (*samādhi-siddhiḥ*), the production of *samādhi,* yogic trance.

11. But the production of *samādhi* is by the lower form of devotion.—20

'Contemplation' there (in the aphorism of Patañjali cited above) mean only the lower form of devotion, and not the higher. By the lower form of devotion is the production of *samādhi.* Hence there is also no contradiction with the Smṛti (i.e., *Yogasūtram* of Patañjali). And (to the same purport) there are in the very same work the concluding words (of the section on the Lord): "His name is *Praṇava*" (I. 27). "Its repetition, and contemplation of the object (i.e., the Lord) denoted by it (make the mind steady)" (I.28).—11

हेया रागत्वादिति चेन्नोत्तमास्पदत्वात् सङ्गवत् ।। १ । २ । १२ ।।

हेया (*heyā*), to be avoided. रागत्वात् (*rāga-tvāt*), as being an affection. इति (*iti*), thus. चेत् (*cet*), if. न (*na*), no. उत्तमास्पदत्वात् (*uttama-āspada-tvāt*), as having an object which is laudable. सङ्गवत् (*saṅga-vat*), as association.

12. (If you say that devotion) is to be avoided, since it is an affection, (we reply). No, because it has an object which is laudable, as (is the case with) 'association'.—21

This aphorism proceeds from the introduction of the *Yogaśāstra* (in the preceding aphorism). It may be said that devotion also is certainly to be avoided by one who desires *mukti,* because there is present in it without modification the characteristic of that affection which is mentioned in the *Yogaśāstra* (*Yogasūtram,* II.3, as one of the five 'afflictions'). Thus there is the aphorism: "(Nescience, egoism), affection, aversion, and love of life are the afflictions." If you say so, we reply, it should not be said so, because devotion has an its object something which is laudable, that is to say, because it has the Supreme Lord as its object. For (according to Patañjali) affection is not to be avoided merely on the ground of its being affection, but only on the ground of its being an affection which clings to the world. As for example, association is not to avoided merely on the ground of its being association, but on the ground of its being an association with wicked people. So is the case here. Thus when it is said that devotion to God is to be avoided, because it is an affection, the special conditions that must be present will be that it tends to cause attachment to the world and that it is not subserving the end of *mukti.*

Nor is this devotion devoid of the illuminating presence of *sattva*; for, in such texts as "those possessing the nature of *sattva*, worship the gods" (*Gītā,* XVII.4), it is declared that it is connected with *sattva.*—12

तदेव कर्मिज्ञानियोगिभ्यः आधिक्यशब्दात् ।। १ । २ । १३ ।।

तत् (*tat*), this, worship, devotion. एव (*eva*), certainly. कर्मिज्ञानियोगिभ्यः (*karmi-jñāni-yogi-bhyaḥ*), to the performers of sacrificial act, the followers of knowledge and the followers of yoga. आधिक्यशब्दात् (*ādhikya-śabdāt*), from the revelation of superiority.

13. This certainly (is supreme), since there is the revelation about its superiority to the performers of sacrificial acts, to the followers of knowledge, and to the followers of yoga.—22

The very same worship is the principal thing or the character of being principal belongs to devotion. This is ascertained in every way indeed, since it is thus revealed:

"The *yogī* is higher than the ascetics, he is counted higher than even those who follow knowledge.

The *yogī* is higher than those who perform sacrificial acts; therefore, O

Arjuna, be thou a *yogī*.
And of all *yogīs,* whosoever with his (inner) soul intent on me
In full belief worships me, he is accounted by me the most devoted."
(Cowell, *Gītā,* VI.46, 47)

Here it is to be understood that the superiority of the persons qualified, which is due to the superiority of their respective qualifications such as asceticism, etc., is successive (i.e., of the one to the other in the order of their mention). (For) surely the superiority of a subsidiary to its principal is not established. Hence it follows that devotion is the principal.—13

(It might be suggested that the above revelation is a mere *arthavāda,* and that what is regarded as a subsidiary is also competent to produce the desired result, i.e., *mukti,* and as such possesses superiority also). With a view to avoid the appearance of superiority (in the subsidiary), also by means of the lessons of the Revelation, the author reads:

प्रश्ननिरूपणाभ्यामाधिक्यसिद्धेः ।। १ । २ । १४ ।।

प्रश्ननिरूपणाभ्याम् (*praśna-nirūpaṇa-bhyām*), by question and answer. आधिक्यसिद्धेः (*ādhikya-siddheḥ*), from the proof of superiority (of devotion).

14. (The revelation cited above is not an *arthavāda*), because of the proof of the superiority (of devotion) by means of question and answer.—23

Here the whole of the twelfth chapter (of the *Gītā*) is an example of this method of proof. The question is in the form:

"They who in faith worship thee, thus constantly devoted to thee,
And they who worship the indestructible and the unmanifested, which of these knows most of yoga?" (Cowell)

The answer is as follows:

"They who fixing their mind on me, worship me, ever devoted,
Endowed with the highest belief, they are counted by me the most devoted.
But they who worship the indestructible, the indescribable, and the unmanifested,
The all-prevading, the inconceivable, the unchangeable, the unmoved, the permanent.
Restraining all their senses, having equanimity of mind towards all,
These verily attain me being intent on the welfare of all.
Their labour is the greater who fix their thoughts on the unmanifested.

The path of the unmanifested is with difficulty obtained by embodied beings.
But they who are intent on me, having transferred all their actions to me,
And worship me, contemplating me with unfaltering concentration,
To them a deliverer from the sea of death and the world
I shall ere long be, son of Pṛthā, as their thoughts are fixed on me."

(Cowell, *Gītā,* XII.1-7)

As this question and answer proves the supriority of devotion, the passage cannot he considered to be an *arthavāda.* For it is well-known that the form of question and answer is for the purpose of ascertainment, and not for the purpose of commendation. It is only an excess of labour and trouble that is entailed by the pursuit of subsidiary itself (apart from the principal to which it is subservient).—14

The author proceeds to expel the demon in the form of the apprehension which may arise from the mention of the word 'belief' (in the above passage), namely that devotion is a kind of belief.

नैव श्रद्धा तु साधारण्यात् ।। १ । २ । १५ ।।

न (*na*), not. एव (*eva*), by any means. श्रद्धा (*śraddhā*), belief. तु (*tu*), but. साधारण्यात् (*sādhāraṇyāt*), applying it universally.

15. (Devotion should) not (be supposed to be a kind of) belief, by applying (the term, devotion) universally.—24

Devotion should by no means be apprehended to be a form of belief, because belief is a subsidiary of sacrificial acts alone. Not so is devotion to the Lord.—15

तस्यां तत्त्वे चाऽनवस्थानात् ।। १ । २ । १६ ।।

तस्यां (*tasyāṃ*), in this i.e., devotion. तत्त्वे (*tat-tve*), that, i.e., the characteristic of being a subsidiary of belief, being found. च (*ca*), and. अनवस्थानात् (*an-avasthānāt*), from infinite regression.

16. (Devotion cannot be a form of belief), also because, since (in that case) devotion in the form of belief would be a subsidiary of belief, there would be infinite regression.—25

For, "He who worships Me with belief* is accounted by Me the most devoted." (*Gītā,* VI.47)

*"Here 'belief' is subsidiary to 'faith' according to the rule 'that which characterizes the agent is a subsidiary part of the ceremony to be performed'; as in the injunction 'let him who desires heaven offer the sacrifice', where the desire of heaven is considered to be subsidiary."—Cowell

Such is the Śruti. Since in this verse it is found that belief is a subsidiary of devotion which is, you say, a form of belief, there would ensue infinite regression, as belief then would be without a subsidiary. Otherwise, if you maintain that belief also would have a subsidiary, viz., a different belief, there would still arise the same infinite regression (as you will have to imagine subsidiary belief in turn *ad infinitum*). Therefore, (if we are to avoid this infinite regression), as (for the same reason) in the case of the opening verses of a ceremony which do not require any opening verses at their commencement, and as also in the case of the rinsing of the mouth (preliminary to a ceremony) which does not require a preliminary rinsing for itself, so in the present case belief would not but a subsidiary of devotion. (But this is in contradiction to the Śruti quoted above which declares belief to be a subsidiary of devotion. Devotion therefore cannot be a form of belief.)

And another reason why devotion and belief cannot be treated as identical is their separate mention in such phrases as "endowed with belief and devotion".—16

ब्रह्मकाण्डं तु भक्तौ तस्यानुज्ञानाय सामान्यात् ।। १ । २ । १७ ।।

ब्रह्मकाण्डं (*brahma-kāṇḍam*), the portion of the Veda treating of Brahman. तु (*tu*), but. भक्तौ (*bhaktau*), in respect of devotion. तस्य (*tasya*), its. अनुज्ञानाय (*anujñānāya*), from the point of knowledge. सामान्यात् (*sāmānyāt*), being the same.

17. But the Brahma-kāṇḍa (is directed) to devotion (as its end), since, as a source of knowledge, it does not differ (from the Pūrva-kāṇḍa).—26

The aphorism is addressed to one who thinks that, if knowledge were not superior to devotion, the latter protion of the Veda would not have been universally known as the Jñāna-kāṇḍa, i.e., the portion treating of knowledge (as opposed to the early portion which treats of *karma,* i.e., sacrificial acts, etc.). The Brahma-kāṇḍa is revealed for the purpose of devotion, and not for the purpose of knowledge; since the making known of what was previously unknown is the common characteristics of both the *kāṇḍas* (so that both would equally be Jñāna-kāṇḍa). Nor is it possible to regard this latter portion as laying down rules for the acquisition of knowledge, wherefore, owing to knowledge being its principal aim, it might have been described as Jñāna-kāṇḍa. Therefore, the idea that it is a Jñāna-kāṇḍa is a mistake. But it is really Brahma-kāṇḍa. Hence has it been aphorised:

"Now, then, there is a wish to know Brahman" (*Brahmasūtram*, I.i.1). This, therefore, is a Bhakti-kāṇḍa, as devotion is the object it aims at.—17

Thus ends the second lecture of the first chapter in the commentary on the One Hundred Aphorisms of Śāṇḍilya composed by the most learned teacher Svapneśvara.

Chapter II

The Means of Devotion

Lecture I: The Internal Means

This devotion is not to be produced directly by an effort. For its production other means are to be looked for. Of these means, the intimate or internal one is knowledge; the extraneous ones are the lower form of devotion, etc. For the discrimination of these means is the commencement of the second chapter.

बुद्धिहेतुप्रवृत्तिराविशुद्धेरवघातवत् ।। २ ।१ ।१ ।।

बुद्धिहेतुप्रवृत्तिः (*buddhi-hetu-pravṛttiḥ*), practice of the means of knowledge. आविशुद्धेः (*ā-viśuddheḥ*), till (complete) purification (of the mind). अवघातवत् (*avaghāta-vat*), like the shelling (or rice).

1. The practice of the means of knowledge (is to be kept up till the complete purification of the mind, as (in the case of) the shelling of rice.—27

'Knowledge means certain knowledge about Brahman. Although this cannot be produced by efforts, still the practice of the means thereof, such as hearing, pondering, meditating, etc., is necessary for its production. Here the doubt arises whether one is to exert once only, following the maxim "the meaning of the *śāstra* is fulfilled when once performed", or whether one is to exert till firmness of devotion is achieved. To this it is replied: The practice of the means is necessary till the complete purification of devotion. Just as, for example, it is the intention of the injunction, "he shells the rice", that the act of shelling is to be performed till the rice is completely cleared of its husk, so, its utility having been observed, one must strive to practise knowledge and the other means till the removal of all impurity of mind.—1

If it be urged that it does not follow that there is to be the practice of those acts which are subsidiary to these subsidiaries of devotion,—to this is the reply:

तदङ्गानां च ।। २ ।१ ।२ ।।

तदङ्गानां (*tat-aṅgānām*), of their subsidiaries, auxiliaries. च (*ca*), also.

2. And of their subsidiaries also.—28

"Of their subsidiaries," i.e., of obedience to preceptors, investigation of arguments not in contradiction to the Veda, self-restraint, and so forth, also the practice is necessary. For, subsidiaries which are disorganised in their subordinate parts, are not able to contribute to the cause of the principal, just as the general is useless without his army remaining in perfect organisation.—2

Next is considered the question of the purification of the object of knowledge.

तामैश्वर्य्यपरां काश्यपः परत्वात् ।। २ । १ । ३ ।।

ताम् (*tām*), it, i.e. knowledge. ऐश्वर्य्यपरां (*aiśvarya-parāṃ*), directed to lordliness or majesty. काश्यपः (*kāśyapaḥ*), a sage of that name. परत्वात् (*paratvāt*), being other.

3. Kāśyapa holds that knowledge of lordliness (is the cause of the highest good), from its being other (than the knower).—29

The teacher Kāśyapa considers that 'it' i.e., knowledge, which has as its object a being endowed with the majesty of the Supreme Lord and other attributes, produces the highest good as its fruit. How so? Because this Supreme Being is other than the embodied souls, since for the sake of the knowledge of one's own self there is need for the knowledge of another. In this view there is an absolute difference between the *jīva* and Brahman.—3

आत्मैकपरां बादरायणाः ।। २ । १ । ४ ।।

आत्मैकपरां (*ātmā-eka-parāṃ*), directed to the pure self. बादरायणाः (*bādarāyaṇāḥ*), the sage of that name.

4. Bādarāyaṇa is of opinion that knowledge of the self pure and simple (is the cause of the highest good).—30

The teacher Bādarāyaṇa, again, considers that it is knowledge having the pure self as its object, which is the cause of the highest good. And so there is the aphorism (*Brahmasūtram,* IV.i.3) "But the Masters contemplate on Brahman as the self and teach it so to their pupils." In this view, as the notion that this is *jīva,* that is Brahman, is false, *tattva-jñāna,* knowledge of reality, is the knowledge that there is but oneself which is pure consciousness, and therefore, it is that knowledge which obtains *mukti* as its fruit.—4

उभयपरां शाण्डिल्यः शब्दोपपत्तिभ्याम् ।। २।१।५।।

उभयपरां (*ubhaya-parāṃ*), directed to both, i.e., both lordliness and the self. शण्डिल्यः (*śāṇḍilyaḥ*), sage of that name, not the author of our aphorisms. शब्दोपपत्तिभ्याम् (*śabda-upapatti-bhyām*), from Revelation and reasoning.

5. Śāṇḍilya considers that knowledge of both (lordliness and the self, is the cause of the highest good), in accordance with Revelation and reasoning.—31

The teacher Śāṇḍilya, on the other hand, considers that it is the knowledge of both (which is the cause of the highest good). How so? Because Revelation, i.e., the Veda, says so. After beginning with "All this verily is Brahman; thence it proceeds, therein it disappears, and therein it moves; thus let him worship it with a tranquil mind", the *Chāndogya Upaniṣad* (III.xiv.1-4) disposes of the doubt about the self in the words: "this is myself within my heart, this is Brahman, this shall I obtain, having passed from hence,—I who am sure of this and have no doubt; so says Sāṇḍilya, so says Śāṇḍilya." It thus declares that he who knows both these objects, obtains the fruit of realising Brahman, which is produced by *prema bhakti,* that intense form of devotion called spiritual love of the Lord, directed to Brahman as its object.

Just as in the case of "Babara Prāvāhaṇi desired" (*Taittirīya Saṃhitā,* VII.i.10), there is no contradiction (of the eternal truth of the Veda) by the incorporation of the non-eternal with the eternal (in the above text where the name of Śāṇḍilya is mentioned), for the reference is to a former Śāṇḍilya. In reality, the Veda has the Lord as its maker. This is learnt from the Śruti also:

> "From that sacrifice universal were produced the *Ṛks* and the *Sāmans,*
> Therefrom were produced the metres, the *Yajus* was produced from it."
> (*Ṛgveda,* V.x.90)

Reasoning also proves the point. Brahman is revealed as possessing supreme lordliness and also as constituting the essential form of the *jīva.* Thus there is the Śruti:

> "From whom verily these beings are born, by whom, when born, they live, whom they approach, whom they enter, him do thou seek to know." (*Taittirīya Upaniṣad,* III.i.1)

And so the *Gītā:*

"A portion of Me is, in the animate world, become the *jīva,* eternal." (XV.7)

This being the case, what can destroy what? Therefore, it is only that interpretation of such sentences as "That thou art", according to which both *jīva* and Brahman are established, that is reasonable.—5

वैषम्यादसिद्धमिति चेन्नाभिज्ञानवदवैशिष्ट्यात् ।। २ । १ । ६ ।।

वैषम्यात् (*vaiṣamyāt*), on account of incompatibility. असिद्धम् (*a-siddham*), not proved. इति (*iti*), thus. चेत् (*cet*), if. न (*na*), no. अभिज्ञानवत् (*abhijñāna-vat*), as in the case of recognition. अवैशिष्ट्यात् (*a-vaiśiṣṭyāt*), in the absence of distinctive mark.

6. If (you say that this is) not proved on account of incompatibility, (we reply), no, (this is proved) as is recognition in the absence of the distinctive mark.—32

You may say that this itself, namely that knowledge has both lordliness and the self together in one act as its object, is not proved, on account of their incompatibility; for incompatible is the knowledge that it is an object qualified as not being the creator of the world, etc., in regard to an object qualified as being the creator of the world, etc. We reply that this is not so. For, just as in the case of such recognition as "That is this same Devadatta", "That is I", the knowledge of both together is rendered possible by the fact that co-existence of two things in the same receptacle (thought) takes cognisance of that portion of them which consists in their essential non-difference, without the presence of the distinctive characteristics of the one in the other having its own distinctive characteristics; inasmuch as the knowledge (for the purpose of recognition) of the distinctive characteristics of one thing in another which has its own distinctive characteristics, is a general rule which admits of exceptions.

Is it then your theory, you may ask, that the essential non-difference is brought forward not directly by the objects as specially qualified, but through indirect reference or suggestion by the objects themselves aprat from their special qualifications? We reply, No, because to make known by indirect reference is discreditable, and because the cause of the bringing forward of the thing suggested is not suggestion but the presence of the circumstances which determine it. If it were not so, there might sometimes be the recollection of the thing suggested even without the circumstances determining it to be the thing suggested. Let this suffice.—6

न च क्लिष्टः परः स्यादनन्तरं विशेषात् । । २ । १ । ७ । ।

न (*na*), nor. च (*ca*), again. क्लिष्टः (*kliṣṭaḥ*), subject to affliction. परः (*paraḥ*), the other, the Supreme Lord. स्यात् (*syāt*), would be. अनन्तरं (*an-antaraṃ*), immediately after. विशेषात् (*viśeṣāt*), there being difference.

7. Nor would the Supreme Lord be, (on our theory) subject to affliction, since immediately after (identity) there is a difference.—33

Nor is it possible to say that this (i.e., the identity of the *jīva* and Brahman) being so, the possession of affliction, etc., appertaining to the adjunct of the *jīva,* (i.e., the internal organ), would also be entailed in the case of the Supreme Lord. Because, immediately after the above knowledge of their non-difference, there is the ascertainment of their difference in the form that affliction, etc., have no connection with the self.—7

ऐश्वर्य्यं तथेति चेन्न स्वाभाव्यात् । । २ । १ । ८ । ।

ऐश्वर्य्यं (*aiśvaryam*), lordliness. तथा (*tathā*), likewise. इति (*iti*), thus. चेत् (*cet*), if. न (*na*), no. स्वाभाव्यात् (*svābhāvyāt*), being of his very nature.

8. If (you say that) lordliness will be likewise (excluded from the Supreme Lord, we reply), no, because it is of His very nature.—34

If you say that like affliction, etc., lordliness characterised as His being the Creator, etc., is in the same way excluded from the Supreme Lord, whereas the character of all-pervadingness, having been witnessed in the self, is not (excluded) like affliction, etc., we reply, no, because the characteristic of being the Creator, etc., appertain to the Supreme Lord's own nature. For the character of fire to be hot by nature is never altered. Therefore, the being not natural is the immediate condition of exclusion. Hence although there is obstruction to the attribution of the darkness, etc., detected in the image, to the sun reflected in the mirror, etc., (darkness, etc. not being natural to the sun), there is surely no obstruction to the attribution of roundness, brightness, and other natural characteristics.—8

Well, the lordliness of the Supreme Lord is real; but how is it, you may ask, that affliction, etc., are adventitious to the *jīvas*? The author declares the cause of this difference.

अप्रतिषिद्धं परैश्वर्यं तद्भावाच्च नैवमितरेषाम् । । २ । १ । ६ । ।

अप्रतिषिद्धं (*a-pratiṣiddhaṃ*), unhindered. परैश्वर्यं (*para-aiśvaryaṃ*), lordliness of the Supreme. तद्भावात् (*tat-bhāvāt*), from having His substance. च (*ca*), and. न (*na*), not. एवम् (*evam*), so, i.e., natural. इतरेषाम् (*itareṣām*), of the others, i.e., of the *jīvas.*

9. The lordliness of the Supreme is unhindered, and because the *jīvas* share His substance, affliction, etc., are not natural to them.—35

For, in no (Śruti) whatever is the lordlines of the Supreme Lord interdicted; whereby even that which is established should be excluded. Rather from such texts as "Whose will is truth" (*Chāndogya Upaniṣad,* III.xiv.2), it is learnt that lordliness is His nature. Nor is there any reason for abandoning the attribute that is observed in Him, as there is in the case of the *jīva;* for He is every moment the Lord, He is every moment free. But to the others than the Supreme, i.e., the *jīvas,* affliction, etc., are not thus natural; why? because they share His substance. For this is revealed by such texts as "he attains to the supreme light, he is evolved by his form" (*Chāndogya Upaniṣad*, VIII.iii.4). And this would not be possible, if affliction, etc., were natural to the *jīvas.* It might be possible, again, if affliction, etc., were the nature of Supreme; but this is not so. Therefore, also for the reason that *mukti* defined as Brahma-realisation would otherwise be impossible, (it follows that) *saṃsāra* is caused to the *jīvas* by their adjunct, i.e., the internal organ. Although in the case of the Supreme also, lordliness has *māyā* as its *upādhi* or special condition, still there is never an absolute dissolution of this *upādhi,* (and thus lordliness remains unimpaired). Of the internal organ which are the *upādhis* of the *jīvas,* on the other hand, it is the absolute dissolution that takes place when the higher devotion is produced. But it does not follow that the *māyā* energy of the Lord also at the same time ceases; because, as there is an infinity of the *jīvas,* activity is ever necessary on the part of the Lord for the sake of their *saṃsāra* and their worship. And so the Śruti, "he as it were thinks, he as it were moves", (*Bṛhadāraṇyaka Upaniṣad*, IV.iii.7) and also the Śruti, "now then the declaration, Not this, Not this" (ibid., II.iii.6), etc., have the *jīva* as their object.—9

सर्वानृते किमिति चेन्नैवम्बुद्ध्यानन्त्यात् ।। २।१।१०।।

सर्वानृते (*sarva-anṛte*), on the dissolution of all, i.e., all the internal organs. किम् (*kim*), what, इति (*iti*), thus. चेत् (*cet*), if. न (*na*), not. एवम् (*evam*), so. बुद्ध्यानन्त्यात् (*buddhi-ānantyāt*), from the infinity of the internal organs.

10. (If you ask), on the dissolution of all, what (is the use of

lordliness)? (we reply), not so, owing to the infinity of internal organs.—36

Now, even if *mukti* (of the *jīvas*) is gradual, when there will be the dissolution of all internal organs (one after another), the *upādhi* of the Supreme will only be left; from the absence of any purpose to serve, there will be absolute dissolution of this also; what is the good, then, you may ask, of attributing lordliness as the nature of the Supreme? We reply, it never so happens. Since the number of the internal organs which are the adjuncts of the *jīvas* is infinite, such a time itself will never be. Hence it is right that lordliness should be natural to the Supreme.

Nor is the case for such a time to come made out by the argument that all antecedent non-existence (in other words, potential existences, as of the jar, e.g., before its actual production) cause the production of their opposites (in other words, emergent or actual existences), from their being antecedent non existences, (for if they did not produce their opposites, they would not be antecedent non-existences, but would be absolute non-existences). (For then, however infinite the number of the *jīvas* may be, the antecedent non-existences of their *mukti* are bound to produce their opposites, i.e., *mukti.* This being so, a time will surely come when all the *jīvas* will attain *mukti* and there will be left no necessity for the continuance of the lordliness of the Supreme. So that lordliness cannot be natural to Him.) (In this view it must be held that all antecedent non-existences had once produced their opposites, or that there was a time when none of them produced any effect.) Now, if you say that at one time they had all produced their opposites; we reply, no, since in that case your argument would be inapplicable (since it would then be admitted by you that even after the *jīvas* had once attained *mukti,* they are again, or there were others who are, in a state of bondage). On the other hand, inference of a time in which none of them produced any effect would be absolutely devoid of reason. Otherwise, by the inference that all antecedent non-existences had at a certain time not produced their opposites, an antecedent time would be established in which there was yet no destruction or emergent non-existence.

If you say that such an idea as "May be, I am the *jīva* who will not attain *mukti*" (which is not uncommon) will entail an absence of effort towards *mukti;* we reply, even if there be uncertainty as to the fruit, when there is certainty as to devotion being the means, thereof, there should rather be activity towards that means. On the contrary, it will be the certainty as to the *mukti* of all (by the mere operation of the antecedent non-existences of *mukti*), which you advocate, that will entail absence of activity towards the attainment of *mutki.*—10

If lordliness defined as the being the material cause be natural to the Supreme, then this would lead, you may say, to nothing but His being subject to change, as is the case with clay, etc. To this it is replied:

प्रकृत्यन्तरालादवैकार्यं चित्सत्त्वेनानुवर्त्तमानात् ।। २ । १ । ११ ।।

प्रकृत्यन्तरालात् (*prakṛti-antarālāt*), from the medium of *Prakṛti* matter. अवैकार्यं (*a-vaikāryaṃ*), immutability, चित्सत्त्वेन (*cit-sattvena*), by existence in the form of the intelligent. अनुवर्त्तमानात् (*anu-varttamānāt*), from enterning, from being present.

11. Since *Prakṛti* is the medium, the Supreme is not subject to change from entering *Prakṛti* as a manifestation of the Intelligent.—37

What is called *Prakṛti* is the material cause of all insensate effects. This is subject to change: but not so Brahman. The Supreme's being the creator, etc., consists in existence which is a form of the manifestation of Brahman and in his entering into *Prakṛti.* Nor is it possible to say that *Prakṛti* itself is existence, because this would entail the non-existence of the *jīvas,* as they are other than *Prakṛti.* Therefore, the Supreme has as His nature the being the Creator, etc., through the medium of *māyā* energy characterised as *Prakṛti;* hence He is not subject to change. For a magician, creating by magic, does not become the effect of his magic. (Similarly, the Supreme, creating by *māyā,* does not become an effect of *māyā,* and therefore, subject to change.)

Although by reason of the identity of cause and effect, the very fact of being an effect means the being changed, and although liability to change in this sense surely exists in the Supreme, yet He is not subject to change by a change of essential form as in the case of milk (becoming curds), etc.

Or, we may explain that He is not subject to change any more than the potter's stick is in reference to the jar, since it is not the cause of any other change than that produced in the jar.

Hence it is said "through the medium of *Prakṛti*".—11

If then *māyā* is the material cause of the world, the world is founded on *māyā* alone; how then, you may ask, is the foundation of the world on Brahman established by the Śruti "on Him is all founded" (*Taittirīya Khila Upaniṣad*)? To this the reply is as follows.

तत्प्रतिष्ठा गृहपीठवत् ।। २ । १ । १२ ।।

तत्प्रतिष्ठा (*tat-pratiṣṭhā*), foundation on Him. गृहपीठवत् (*gṛhapīṭhavat*), like a stool, in a house.

12. Foundation on Him (is not incompatible), as in the case of a stool in a house.—38

On Him, i.e., on Brahman, even the foundation of the changes of *māyā* is not incompatible, "as in the case of a stool in a house": Just as even of a man seated on a stool inside a house, we say, "he is seated in the house," "he is seated on a stool," so it is here also.—12

If so, then, is not, you may ask, Brahman otherwise established as being *Prakṛti* itself? To this it is replied:

मिथोऽपेक्षणादुभयम् ।। २ । १ । १३ ।।

मिथः (*mithaḥ*), mutual. अपेक्षाणात् (*apekṣaṇāt*), from requiring. उभयम् (*ubhayam*), both, i.e., both Brahman and *Prakṛti.*

13. As they mutually need each other, both (Brahman and *Prakṛti* are causes).—39

Brahman and *Prakṛti,* both of them, are causes. Because the intelligent (Brahman) and the non-intelligent (*Prakṛti*) are mutually needed by each other for the sake of their own knowledge and also for being the subject of their respective powers, which of them can overlook and other?—13

The author now declares an enumeration of categories in order to simplify their use or employment in his work.

चेत्याचितोर्न तृतीयम् ।। २ । १ । १४ ।।

चेत्याचितोः (*cetyācitoḥ*), beside the knowable and the knower. न (*na*), no. तृतीयम् (*tṛtīyam*), third.

14. There is no third beside the knowable and the knower.—40

Knowable is *Prakṛti,* knower is Brahman,—beside them there is in this treatise no other third principle recognised; such is the meaning. If you say that the existence or non-existence of a third does not matter, we reply that what the author means is that to be the knower is denied to what is different from Brahman, and that to be the knowable is denied to what is diffcrent from *Prakṛti.* —14

Now, you may say that if there is no connection between *Prakṛti* and *Puruṣa* (Brahman), there is an end of all effects, while, on the other hand, if there is a connection, this itself is the third (which is denied). To this the author replies:

युक्तौ च सम्परायात् ।। २।१।१५ ।।

युक्तौ (*yuktau*), united. च (*ca*), and. सम्परायात् (*samparāyāt*), from beginninglessness.

15. And (both are) united together, because (they are) beginningless.—41

The word 'mutually' follows from aphorism 39. They, i.e., *Prakṛti* and *Puruṣa* under reference, are of the form of correlatives to each other; it is not that there is between them some extraneous connection; why? "from beginninglessness," i.e., from the very fact that they are beginningless. And thus in the *Gītā* (XIII.20): "*Prakṛti* and also *Puruṣa,* know that both of them are beginningless."

Now, if you say, let there be a different connection which is also beginningless, we reply, no, because, as the insensate and non-insensate are the alternatives, they do not admit of a third.—15

But *Prakṛti* is certainly false, because, it is of the form of *māyā,* as appears from such Śrutis as "Let him know that *Prakṛti* is *māyā,* and that Maheśvara is he to whom *māyā* belongs" (*Śvetāśvatara Upaniṣad,* IV.10); how is it therefore, you may ask, declared as the category of the knowable? To this the author replies—

शक्तित्वान्नानृतं वेद्यम् ।। २।१।१६ ।।

शक्तित्वात् (*śakti-tvāt*), from being is power. न (*na*), not. अनृतं (*anṛtaṃ*), false. वेद्यम् (*vedyam*), the knowable.

16. The knowable is not false because it is a power.—42

The 'knowable', i.e., *Pradhāna* (another name of *Prakṛti*), 'not false', does not deserve to be false; why? because of the very fact that it is a power. For a magician, without the power of magic, has no power for the creation of a given extraneous thing. Moreover, the Śruti, "But how gentle youth, could it be so that the existent were produced from the non-existent?" (*Chāndogya Upaniṣad,* VI.ii.2) which declares the reality of the cause inferred by the reality of the effect, reveals the existence of all, and not falseness. There is, again, always in the creation of the Lord the necessity for a concomitant cause corresponding (to the thing created, i.e., for *Prakṛti* which therefore cannot be false), because it is creation by an intelligent being, just as in the creation of the magician (there is the necessity for magic as a concomitant cause corresponding in nature to the magician's creation).

Nor is a different concomitant cause furnished, as you may suggest, by *adṛṣṭa* (merit and demerit), etc., because it is simpler to assume the necessity for a single power (i.e., *Prakṛti,* instead of an indefinite number of *adṛṣṭa,* etc.), and because there is no evidence that *adṛṣṭa* is the cause of anything except worldly experience and the means thereof. Again, as a number of these other causes will inevitably wander together in all effects, there is proof of one, eternal concomitant power. On the other hand, the supposition of many other causes subsidiary to this one, operating towards the fruit, is not an offence against the law of parsimony. An elaboration of this point will be found in the third chapter.—16

The discussion (in aphorism 43) started as a digression is thus dismissed. The author now pursues the matter under consideration.

तत्परिशुद्धिषुश्च गम्या लोकवल्लिङ्गेभ्यः ।। २ । १ । १७ ।।

तत्परिशुद्धिः (*tat-pariśuddhiḥ*), the purity thereof, i.e., of devotion. च (*ca*), and. गम्या (*gamyā*), to be inferred. लोकवत् (*loka-vat*), as in common life. लिङ्गेभ्यः (*liṅgebhyaḥ*), by means of marks or signs.

17. And its complete purity is to be inferred by means of marks as in common life.—43

Although devotion is no doubt an object of sense-perception (cf. internal organ which is mind) through such cognitions as "I worship", "I have affection", etc., just as through such cognitions as "I know", "I will", etc., knowledge and volition are objects of sense-perception; still its complete purity, characterised by being informed with deeper and stronger impressions, is not possible to know through sense-perception, just as in the case of the authoritativeness of knowledge.* Therefore, its ascertainment is by means of marks only, as in common life. Just as in common life the greater or less degrees of affection are inferred by means of its physical expressions such as tears, horripilation, etc., when one listens to discourses, etc., about the object of affection; so is it here.—17

The author next declares that not only are there marks as in life, but that such marks are abundantly obtained also from the recorded recollection of great sages.

*"The Prabhākara school of the Mīmāṃsā hold that knowledge is an object of internal perception, and its correctness (or authoritativeness, *pramāṇya*) is cognised by the same act of cognition as the knowledge itself. There is (1) the perception of the object, i.e., 'this is a jar'; (2) the consciousness of this perception, i.e., 'I perceive the jar'; (3) simultaneously with (2) the cognition of the truth of the perception. The Nyāya holds that the three steps are successive and the last is gained by inference, not by direct consciousness. If it were gained by direct consciousness, there could be no such thing as doubt."—Cowell

सम्मानबहुमानप्रीतिविरहेतरविचिकित्सामहिमख्यातितदर्थप्राणस्थानतदीयतासर्वतद्भावा-प्रातिकूल्यादीनि च स्मरणेभ्यो बाहुल्यात् ।। २ । १ । १८ ।।

सम्मानबहुमानप्रीतिविरहेतरविचिकित्सामहिमख्यातितदर्थप्राणस्थानतदीयतासर्वतद्भावा-प्रातिकूल्यादीनि (*sammāna-bahumāna-prīti-viraha-itaravicikitsā-mahimakhyāti-tadarthaprāṇasthāna-tadīyatā-sarvatadbhāva-aprātikūlya-ādīni*), honour, esteem, delight, forlornness, doubt as regards others, celebration of glory, preservation of life for his sake, sense of belonging to him, his omnipresence, resignation to his will, etc. च (*ca*), and. स्मरणेभ्यः (*smaraṇebhyaḥ*), from the Recollections, the Smṛtis. बाहुल्यात् (*bāhulyāt*), in plenty.

18. And from the Recollections (are obtained) in abundance such marks as honour, esteem, delight, forlornness, doubt as regards others, celebration of glory, preservation of life for his sake, sense of belonging to him, his omnipresence, resignation to his will, etc.—44

i. 'Honour', as in the case of Arjuna:

"To rise up before Kṛṣṇa, the winner of wealth (Arjuna), in whatever circumstances,
Never forgets, being of virtuous soul, with devotion and with love."
(*Mahābhārata,* Droṇa Parva, I.2822)

ii. 'Esteem', as in the case of Ikṣvāku:

"Through fondness for his name, to the deer and lotus looking like him,
Even to the cloud which had his colour, the king showed esteem."
(*Nṛsiṃha Purāṇa,* XXV.22)

iii. 'Delight', as in the case of Vidura:

"What delight, O lotus-eyed, I feel from thy coming as its cause,
Why should it be told thee who art the inner soul of all?"
(*Mahābhārata,* Udyoga Parva, LXXXVIII.3114)

iv. 'Forlornness', as in the case of the milkmaids:

"Sayest thou, we should not talk thus in the presence of our superiors?
What can superiors do for us who are burned with the fire of separation?"
(*Viṣṇu Purāṇa,* V.xviii.22)

v. 'Doubt as regards others', as in the case of the inhabitants of Śvetadvīpa, who even seeing that it was Nārada who arrived, felt his presence as a hindrance to their worship of Viṣṇu. As also in the case of Upamanyu:

"Fain would I be even a worm or a grasshopper, at Śaṅkara's command,
Rather than desire even the three worlds, if given, Indra, by thee."
(*Mahābhārata,* Anuśāsana Parva, I.7077)

vi. 'Celebration of glory', as in the case of Yama:

"Addressed Yama the sinful one, in hell tormented:
Why not worshipped by thee the god Keśava, the killer of sorrow?"
(*Nṛsiṃha Purāṇa,* VIII.21)

"Looking at his emissary, noose in hand, whispers Yama in his ear:
Avoid thou those in Madhusūdana reposed: lord am I of other men, but not of Vaiṣṇavas." (*Viṣṇu Purāṇa,* III.vii.14)

vii. 'Preservation of life for his sake', as in the case of Hanumān:
He himself has declared:

"As long as in the world shall circulate thy story purifying the hearts of men,
Shall I remain on the earth so long, obeying the command of thee."
(*Rāmāyaṇa,* Uttara Kāṇḍa, CVII.31)

Or, 'preservation of life for his sake' may mean the preservation of life by Nārada and others even after they had accomplished all their ends, simply for the sake of worshipping Him. Hence there is the Śruti: "To whom all the gods, those who seek *mukti,* and also the reciters of the Veda do obeisance." (*Nṛsiṃhatāpanī,* khaṇḍa VI)

viii. 'Sense of belonging to him', as in the case of Uparicara Vasu:

"His kingdom and his wealth, his wife and so his chariot too,
Regards he always, all is of the Lord."
(*Mahābhārata,* Śānti Parva, CCCXXXVII.12718)

ix. 'His omnipresence' in all beings, as is well-known in the case of Prahlāda. Declared also by Prahlāda himself.

"Thus in beings one and all devotion which wavers not,
Should the wise have knowing Hari is all." (*Viṣṇu Purāṇa,* I.xix.9)

x. 'Resignation to his will', as in the case of Bhīṣma, even when the Lord approached to kill him. By Bhīṣma himself it has been declared,

"Come, lord of the gods, home of the world,
Adoration to thee, bearing in thy hand bow, club, and sword,
Fell me by force, O ruler of the world, from the chariot with pennant flying,

Thou who marvellous prowess in battle showest."

(*Mahābhārata,* Bhīṣma Parva, LVIII.2604)

From the word 'etc.' the actions of Uddhava, Akrūra, and others are to be understood.

Although this, i.e., reference to marks, has been mentioned in "because it is the opposite of hatred" (aphorism 6), still the distinction (of the present from the previous declaration) is that there it was mentioned as a mark of affection, whereas here it is mentioned as a mark of the complete purity of deed devotion.—18

But amongst those who have affection for their master, hatred, jealousy, etc., are felt by those who receive a less degree of his favour, towards those who receive a greater portion of it; if you then ask, are these also the signs? the author replies, no.

द्वेषादयस्तु नैवम् ।। २ । १ । १६ ।।

द्वेषादय: (*dveṣa-ādayaḥ*), hatred, etc. तु (*tu*), but. न (*na*), not. एवम् (*evam*), so.

19. But hatred, etc., are not so.—45

i.e., from their very incompatibility, as has been declared by the divine Vyāsa:

"Neither anger, nor envy, nor greed, nor any wicked thought takes place in righteous people devoted to *Puruṣottama*."

(*Mahābhārata,* Anuśāsana Parva, CXLIX.769)

In the case of Śiśupāla, on the other hand, the order of evolution was just as follows: from hatred, constant remembrance; thence supreme devotion; thence *mukti.*—19

Now, these marks of devotion that are recollected, generally relate to the incarnations of the Lord as its object; but devotion, because it is, as you hold, to be produced from the knowledge of Brahman, should, you may say, properly have the All-Full (i.e., the Supreme Lord, and not His incarnations) as its object. The doubt having been thus raised, the author declares the conclusion (of the discussion on this doubt).

तद्वाक्यशेषात् प्रादुर्भावेष्वपि सा ।। २ । १ । २० ।।

तत् (*tat*), therefore. वाक्यशेषात् (*vākyāśeṣāt*), from the summing up, from the concluding sentences, of the section. प्रादुर्भावेषु (*prādurbhāveṣu*), in respect of manifestations. अपि (*api*), also. सा (*sā*), devotion.

20. Therefore, from the summing up, (it is seen that) the higher

devotion (arises) in respect of the manifestations also.—46

'Sā', the higher devotion, may also have the manifested Self as its object. How do you know this? "From the summing up." For the purpose of the subject proposed in "The worshippers of the gods go to the gods, my worshippers go to me also" (*Gītā,* VII.23), the argument is logically summed up in the denunciation of devotion to other gods in:

"Whoever devotee wishes to worship whatsoever from with faith,
To them respectively I ordain unshaken faith in those forms."

(*Gītā,* VII.21)

Here the object in view would have been fulfilled by saying this much that "whoever devotee . . . whatsoever (deities)." But the text has gone so far as to refer to 'form'. It is therefore inferred that devotion is also directed to the form (manifestation or incarnation) as its proper object. It is also devotion that the section treats of.—20

जन्मकर्मविदश्चाजन्मशब्दात् ।। २ । १ । २१ ।।

जन्मकर्मविदः (*janma-karma-vidaḥ*), of the knower of birth and action. च (*ca*), and. आजन्म (*ā-janma*), cessation of birth. शब्दात् (*śabdāt*), from the Revelation.

21. And of one who knows (His) birth and action, there is no further birth according to Revelation.—47

'Birth', the Lord's assumption of a body is for the sake of such acts as the production of the Veda, destruction of the demons, showing himself to the devotees, which cannot be performed without a body. And 'action' is such as the production of the Veda, etc. These secure as their fruit the non-existence of birth after death to him who knows the truth about them. As, for instance, declares the Lord:

"My birth and action divine who knows in truth,
Leaving body he is born no more, but goes to Me, O Arjuna."

(*Gītā,* IV.9)

Nor does it follow that immortality is the direct fruit of the knowledge of His birth and action. But through the abolition of the impurity of mind, which results from it, this knowledge, by producing that higher devotion which has for its object the Supreme Lord as conditioned by birth and action, comes to produce non-existence of birth as the fruit. Therefore, it is learnt from the Revelation itself that the higher devotion may have as its object the Lord appearing as an incarnation.—21

तच्च दिव्यं स्वशक्तिमात्रोद्भवात् ।। २ । १ । २२ ।।

तत् (*tat*), that, i.e., birth and action. च (*ca*), and. दिव्यं (*divyaṃ*), divine. स्वशक्तिमात्रोद्भवात् (*sva-śakti-mātra-udbhavāt*), from production solely by his own power.

22. And His birth and action are divine, as their production is solely by His own power.—48

"My birth and My action are divine," (says the *Gītā*, IV.9). Here what does divineness imply? It cannot imply that these are produced through merit, because, there is in Him an absence of contact with merit, as there is no proof that *adṛṣṭa* (merit and demerit) belongs to Him. Nor can it imply that these are produced in heaven, for then the character of divineness would not apply to His birth in the world of our earth. But it implies that like the embodiment of the *jīva,* His body is not produced from the five elements as its material causes; but is, on the contrary, produced by His own *māyā* power. Hence there is the declaration of the Lord to Nārada in the Mokṣa Dharma section of the *Mahābhārata* (CCCXLI.12909):

"*Māyā* this is created by Me, that thou seest Me, Nārada."

So also in the *Gītā* (IV, 6):

"Though I am unborn, of unchangeable essence, though I am the lord of all beings,

Yet entering My own *Prakṛti,* I am born by the form of My *māyā*."

Nor is its not being composed of the elements any bar to its being a body, for to be composed of the elements is invariably necessary only in the case of a body which is to be the seat of worldly experience (caused by *adṛṣṭa,* and *adṛṣṭa,* as stated above, does not exist in the case of the incarnations).

Now, if you say that its being the seat of worldly experience is the very thing which constitutes its being a body, (and that what is not so, is not a body), we reply, no, since it is simpler to hold that its being a body consists in its being the basis or support of exertion. The being an exertion is a particular *jāti* or generic property belonging to the class of action; and not that action as such is exertion, as in that case we shall have to apply the term to the action, i.e., movement or change, taking place in a dead body. Nor does the being an exertion consists in its being an action produced by direct volition, as in that case we shall have to predicate in the case of a pot and the like that they exert, since all action is produced by the direct volition of the Supreme Lord. And thus by the argument which enables us to know the nature of the body assumed by the Supreme Lord, there is also proof of the exertion appearing in that body; and so we leave the discussion here.

Nor is the number of *tattvas* or elementary principles exceeded by the proof of the body of the Supreme Lord; because, like a pot and the like, it will not be an elementary principle at all, inasmuch as it does not serve as the material cause of the universe, nor again does it serve as. The prototype of the sense-organs.*—22

But when He has no purpose of His own to accomplish, being all-full, how does He engage in activity? Such an enquiry being possible, the author declares:

मुख्यं तस्य हि कारुण्यम् ।। २।१।२३।।

मुख्यं (*mukhyaṃ*), primary. तस्य (*tasya*), his. हि (*hi*), for. कारुण्यम् (*kāruṇyam*), kindness, compassion.

23. His compassion (which is) primary, (is the cause of His activity).—49

For, in common life men call them compassionate who exert themselves for the destruction of the sufferings of others without any ulterior motive. But this application of the word to them is not in its primary sense; for it is not possible that the destruction of suffering by them should be without any ulterior thought, since their exertion is for the destruction of the pain caused to them by pity, or at any rate, for the sake of attaining merit. Nor, again, would be primary sense of the word "compassionate" be preserved if it is applied to one who exerts himself for the mere destruction of the suffering of others (mere destruction, i.e., destruction without the qualification of being without any ulterior thought) because men do not call one compassionate who is influenced by the ulterior thought of thereby gaining wealth, etc. But it is to the Lord alone who

*"Śāṇḍilya holds that Kṛṣṇa is really a form of the Supreme Brahman (see Comm. on aph. 52); but his body is not a separate primary principle (*tattva*) from the acknowledged 26 of the Vedānta as it is not a *tattva* at all. The 26 *tattvas* are divided first into two great classes, as intelligent (*cit*) and non-intelligent (*acit*). The former includes *Īśvara* and the individual soul, the second all the rest. But the second is in turn divided into general (*vyāpaka*) and special (*vyāpya*): the special are the five elements, the five *tanmātras*, and the eleven senses and organs; the general are matter (i.e., *Īśvara*'s *māyā* power), intellect, and egoism (see comm. on aph. 87). The special spring from the general, as their material cause; and in turn themselves produce all the different individual existences (as pots, etc.) in the world. But the divine body of Kṛṣṇa is not like the special *tattvas*, as nothing in the gross world springs from it; nor can it be like the general *tattvas*, because these are the material causes of the elements, senses, organs, etc., but this divine body is not the material cause of anything. (Cf. the *Tattvakaumudī* in its comm. on *Sāṅkhyakārikā*, aphorism 3, where it is shown that such effects, as pots, etc. cannot be called *tattvas*)".—Cowell

destroys the afflictions of others without any ulterior thought, that compassion belongs in its primary sense. The very same application of the word, compassion, that is made to Him, is made in a secondary sense to those who seek to serve other purposes by their exertion towards the destruction of the sufferings of others. It follows therefore that His activity proceeds from His own compassion, having regard at the same time to the *adṛṣṭa* that will be produced thereby.—23

But since there is by such texts as e.g., "amongst men, the king" (*Gītā,* X.27), the declaration that all *vibhūtis,* glories or pre-eminent manifestations of the power of the Lord, (as distinguished from His incarnations), are also of the form of the Lord, would not, you may ask, *mukti* result also from devotion to the king, etc.? To this the author replies.

प्राणित्वान्नविभूतिषु । । २ । १ । २४ । ।

प्राणित्वात् (*prāṇi-tvāt*), from being connected with *prāṇa* or life-breath. न (*na*), not. विभूतिषु (*vibhūtiṣu*), to the glories or pre-eminent manifestations of the power of the Lord.

24. (*Mukti* does) not (result from devotion) to the *vibhūtis,* because they are connected with the *prāṇa*.—50

The higher devotion which has as its object the being alone which is unconditioned by the adjuncts of the *jīva,* has *mukti* as its fruit, but not affection for the king, etc., who are connected with the adjuncts of the *jīva* in the shape of the *prāṇa,* the internal organ, etc.—24

द्यूतराजसेवयोः प्रतिषेधाच्च । । २ । १ । २५ । ।

द्यूतराजसेवयोः (*dyūta-rāja-sevayoḥ*), of playing with dice and of worshipping the king. प्रतिषेधात् (*pratiṣedhāt*), from prohibition. च (*ca*), and.

25. And because there is the prohibition of worshipping the king as well as of playing with dice, (the king as a *vibhūti* cannot be identical with the Almighty).—51

In the Dharmaśāstras there is recollected the prohibition of playing with dice and of worshipping the king. There would have been no such prohibition, if the king were identical with the Supreme Lord.—25

वासुदेवेऽपीति चेन्नाकारमात्रत्वात् । । २ । १ । २६ । ।

वासुदेवे (*vāsudeve*), in regard to Vāsudeva, Kṛṣṇa, who is mentioned among the *vibhūtis.* अपि (*api*), also. इति (*iti*), thus. चेत् (*cet*), if. न (*na*), no. आकारमात्रत्वात् (*ākāra-mātra-tvāt*), from being a mere form.

26. If (you say that the same prohibition would apply) to Kṛṣṇa Vāsudeva also, (we reply) no, because (Kṛṣṇa was not a *jīva* like others, but) his was merely the form (in which the Lord himself was present).—52

But there is also the revelation among the *vibhūtis*, viz., "I am Vāsudeva among the Vṛṣṇis" (*Gītā,* X.37); so that like the king, etc., he too, you may say, is not to be regarded as identical with the Supreme Lord, and therefore is not to be worshipped at all. We reply that such is not the case; because it is the supreme Brahman which took the mere form of Kṛṣṇa, as Parāśara declares:

"A man is delivered from all sins who hears the race of Yadu,
Wherein descended the Supreme Brahman called Viṣṇu in human from." (*Viṣṇu Purāṇa,* IV.xi.2)

This would not be so, if Kṛṣṇa were a *jīva.*—26

प्रत्यभिज्ञानाच्च ।। २।१।२७।।

प्रत्यभिज्ञानात् (*prat-abhijñā-nāt,* from recognition. च (*ca*), also.

27. And also from recognition (of Kṛṣṇa as Brahman in the Scriptures, it follows that Kṛṣṇa is Brahman, and therefore to be worshipped with the higher devotion).—53

And the recognition of the Supreme Brahman in the object known as Vāsudeva is found in the Śruti (*Nārāyaṇa Upaniṣad,* Atharvaśiras, VI.4):

"The son of Devakī is Viṣṇu, the destroyer of Madhu is Viṣṇu."
To Nārāyaṇa, present in all beings, one, the cause of all, uncaused, the essence of the Supreme Brahman."

Such recognition is also recollected in the Smṛti. For example, Mārkaṇḍeya said to Yudhiṣṭhira, from the memory of what he had witnessed at the time of a *pralaya* or world-dissolution:

"That God who was beheld by me of old, having eyes long as a lotuspetal,
Is now, O tiger of men, thine own relation, Janārdana."
(*Mahābhārata,* Vana Parva, CLXXXIX.13002)

So again, having heard that the Lord is verily not to be seen even by mean of penances, Janamejaya says:

"Verily the Lord, worshipped by the world, is not to be seen even by penances;

Him have they seen immediately, adorned with the Śrīvatsa mark."
(*Mahābhārata,* Śānti Parva, Mokṣa Dharma, CCCXLV.13325

The word 'also' supplies the further reason why Kṛṣṇa Vāsudeva is to have also attained the fruit of immortality.—27

If you ask, why then has Vāsudeva been celebrated as one of the *vibhūtis,* the author replies:

वृष्णिषु श्रैष्ठ्येन तत् ।।२।१।२८।।

वृष्णिषु (*vṛṣṇiṣu*), among the Vṛṣṇis. श्रैष्ठ्येन (*śraiṣṭhyena*), by reason of superiority, pre-eminence. तत् (*tat*), that, i.e., celebration among the *vibhūtis.*

28. His celebration as a *vibhūti* is by virtue of his pre-eminence among the Vṛṣṇis.—54

The declaration of the *vibhūtis* is solely for the purpose of opening the eyes of the reader to the fact that it is to the Supreme Lord to Whom belongs all pre-eminence mentioned in such passages as "Among the Ādityas I am Viṣṇu" (*Gītā,* X.21), etc., and so too in the case of Vāsudeva: also, the celebration of Vāsudeva among the *vibhūtis* is for the purpose of opening the eyes of the reader to this fact only that He is the most excellent one among the Vṛṣṇis.—28

एवं प्रसिद्धेषु च।।२।१।२६।।

एवं (*evaṃ*), similarly. प्रसिद्धेषु (*prasiddheṣu*), in regard to well-known incarnations. च (*ca*), and.

29. And similarly in regard to well-known incarnations.—55

'Similarly', i.e., in the same way as in the case of Vāsudeva, it should be understood that devotion to the other well-known incarnations such as Varāha, Nṛsiṃha, Vāmana, Rāma, etc., also produces *mukti* as its fruit, owing to these incarnations possessing the characteristic mark of Brahman. Or, the aphorism may mean that 'similarly', i.e., by means of their possessing the characteristic mark of Brahman, the idea of excellence only is to be formed in regard to the objects which have been recited as *vibhūtis* in such passages as "Among the Rudras I am Śaṅkara" (*Gītā,* X.23), etc. For it is declared in the *Skanda Purāṇa*

(Kāśīkhaṇḍa, Pūrvabhāga, XXXVII.181)

"Whoever would declare the difference of Viṣṇu and Rudra, or between Śrī and Gaurī,
That utterance of the erring fool is repugnant to the *śāstra.*"

The proof of Śaṅkara's possessing the characteristic mark of Brahman is abundantly found in the Smṛti, etc.—29

Thus ends the first lecture of the second chapter in the commentary on the One Hundred Aphorisms of Śāṇḍilya composed by the most learned teacher Svapneśvara.

Lecture II: The External Means

The two manifest subsidiaries of Devotion, namely knowledge and yoga, have been declared. Now the secondary forms of Devotion are declared, which become fruitful by way of destroying vices which hinder the development of the higher devotion.

भक्त्या भजनोपसंहाराद्गौण्या परायैतद्धेतुत्वात् ।।२।२।१।।

भक्त्या (*bhaktyā*), by devotion. भजनोपसंहारात् (*bhajana-upasaṃhārāt*), from the conclusion of the topic with worship by devotion. गौण्या (*gauṇyā*), by the secondary devotion. पराय (*parāya*), for the higher devotion. एतद्धेतुत्वात् (*etat-hetu-tvāt*), from being the subsidiary means of it:

1. **From the conclusion (of the topic of the higher devotion in the *Gītā*), with "worship by devotion", (the expression must mean) "worship by the secondary devotion"; (as the secondary devotion is needed for the higher devotion), since it is the subsidiary means thereof.—56**

After reciting or referring to the higher devotion established in the seventh chapter, by the expression, "They worship Me with undiverted minds, having known Me as the origin of all beings, and as the imperishable" (*Gītā,* IX.13), it is next declared in ibid. (IX.14):

"Always celebrating My names and deeds in song, and striving, firm in their vow,
And bowing to Me, with devotion, entering in deep meditation, they serve Me, variously."

Thereafter follows the conclusion of the topic in the declaration,

"But they who worship Me with devotion, are in Me, and I also in them."
(*Gītā,* IX.29)

Hence here, just as in the case of 'Let one sacrifice with *citrā*'* (*Taittirīya Saṃhitā,* II.iv.6), one must contemplate the fruit (higher

*"This alludes to Mīmaṃsā discussion on the text "let him who desires cattle, sacrifice with the *citra.*" A discussion is raised (*Nyāyamālāvistāra,* I.4.3.) as to the meaning of *citra,*—is it merely the name of a sacrifice, so called from the six various objects, honey, ghee, etc. offered in it; or does it mean the spotted she-goat which is the Agniṣomīya victim?

devotion) as residing in the same subject as the worship of which the name is devotion; such is the meaning. For, the use of devotion as a name for worship is obtained from the fact of the word, devotion, having been applied to devotion to the Lord in such texts as "he who has devotion to one (i.e., Me) only, is pre-eminent" (*Gītā,* VII.17), and further, the words *bhakti* and *bhajana* have one and the same sense (both being derived from the same root *bhaj*).

Nor, again, is the higher devotion here enjoined as if it were a fruit which could be produced; because it cannot be so enjoined, as it is not a thing which can be produced by an effort of will (vide aphorism 7). Nor even is its being the cause of the supreme good herein first revealed, as if it were not known before; because the revelation thereof is also found in the same seventh chapter in such declarations as "My devotees go to Me also" (*Gītā,* VII.23). But the significance of the text ("But they who worship Me with devotion, are in Me, and I also in them," *Gītā,* IX.29) is: The necessity for some means for the destruction of the hindrances to the higher devotion, introduces the 'celebration of His names and deeds in song', etc.; these are indicated by the word, devotion, in the instrumental case (in IX.14) in a secondary sense, and their being the means of the higher devotion is enjoined thereby; and then to supplement the injunction by an *arthavāda* or recommendation, a complement is added to the sentence in the words "they are in Me, and I in them also". Otherwise, if you take the word, devotion, as having been used in its primary sense of the higher devotion, the sense would be split in two viz. that worship is to be performed with devotion, and that by worship there will be the rest in Me, (and the sense conveyed would contradict the established fact that the fruit, *mukti* results direct from the higher devotion).

As celebration of the names and deeds of the Lord and other acts are only the means of devotion, the secondary application of the word, devotion, to them, as in the case of "ghee verily is length of life" (*Taittirīya Saṃhitā,* II.iii.2), can be easily grasped by the suggestion of the primary sense. Or, by the derivation "by these is worshipped", the word devotion is applied to them in the same way as is the word *udbhid,* i.e., that by which

The Mīmaṃsā decides that *citra* here means the name of the sacrifice as in this way the desired fruit (cattle) and the prescribed means (the *citra* sacrifice) will both belong to (or reside in) the same subject, the offerer. If it had meant the spotted she-goat used as a victim in the Agniṣomīya sacrifice, then in the words "let him who desires cattle sacrifice with the spotted she-goat," the fruit would have belonged to the sacrificer but the spotted she-goat would have been a characteristic of the sacrifice, and belonged to it, and thus we should have had *vaiyādhi-karaṇya."*—Cowell something, e.g., cattle, is dug up, applied to the sacrifice so-called (vide *Āśvalāyana Śrautasūtra,* IX.viii). Or, again, the use of the word is secondary, because it is read in the class of words denoting worship by "Four kinds of men worship Me" (*Gītā,* VII.16), as is the case with the word, creation, or because it is associated with the attribute "generous", as the *Gītā* declares: "All these are without exception generous" (VII.18).—1

रागार्थप्रकीर्त्तिसाहचर्याच्चेतरेषाम् ।। २ । २ । २ ।।

रागार्थप्रकीर्त्तिसाहचर्यात् (*rāga-artha-prakṛti-sāhacaryāt*), through association with celebration of His names and deeds in song, the object of which is affection. च (*ca*), and. इतरेषां (*itareṣām*), of the other forms of secondary devotion.

2. The celebration of His names and deeds in song has as its object the production of affection for Him; and since the other forms of secondary devotion are associated with such celebration (in the *Gītā,* IX.14), the same is also their object.—57

For thus it is revealed:

"Well is the world, O lord of the senses, delighted and filled with love at thy praises." (Cowell, *Gītā,* XI.36)

Here it is directly revealed that the celebration of His names and deeds has as its object the stirring up of affection for Him. Since they are associated with it, the same, i.e., the stirring up of affection, is the fruit also of the other forms of secondary devotion as mentioned by such texts as "Always celebrating My names and deeds in song, and striving, firm in their vow." (*Gītā*, IX.14), etc.—2

अन्तराले तु शेषाः स्युरुपास्यादौ च काण्डत्वात् ।। २ । २ । ३ ।।

अन्तराले (*antarāle*), in the interval. तु (*tu*), but. शेषाः (*śeṣāḥ*), the rest. स्युः (*syuḥ*), will be. उपास्यादौ (*upāsya-ādau*), in the texts on the objects of adoration. च (*ca*), and also. काण्डत्वात् (*kāṇḍa-tvāt*), from their being included in the Brahma-kāṇḍa of the Veda.

3. The rest (of the secondary form of devotion) will be found in the inerval; and also in the texts on the objects of adoration, as they form parts of the Brahma-kāṇḍa.—58

Those secondary forms of devotion which are revealed in the interval between "They worship Me with undiverted minds, having known Me as the origin of all beings and as imperishable" (*Gītā,* IX.13) and "Those who worship Me with devotion, are in Me, and I in them also" (*Gītā,* IX.29), are subsidiaries to the higher devotion, just because they are held as by nippers between the two declarations about the higher devotion; such is the import. These secondary froms of devotion are as follows:

"Always celebrating My names in song, and striving, firm in their vow,
And bowing to Me, with devotion, entering in deep meditation, they serve Me, variously." (*Gītā,* IX.14)

"And others too serve Me, sacrificing with the sacrifice of knowledge,
Some in unity, some in plurality, some variously in My manifold character." (Ibid., IX.15)

Similarly,

"Those who serve Me, thinking on nought besides,
To them, ever attached to Me, I preserve and secure prosperity." (Ibid., IX.22)

Similarly,

"Those attached to the gods, go to the gods, those attached to the *pitṛs,* go to the *pitṛs,*
Those sacrificing to the elements, go to the elements, those who sacrifice to Me, go to Me also." (Ibid., IX.25)

"A leaf, a flower, a fruit, or a handful of water whoever offers to Me with devotion,
The same offered in devotion I eat from him whose soul is at rest." (Ibid., IX.26)

Similarly,

"Whatever thou doest, whatever thou eatest, whatever thou offerest in sacrifice, whatever thou givest,
Whatever penance shou doest, O son of Kuntī, give at all over to Me." (Ibid., IX.27)

"Thus shalt thou be delivered from the fruits, good or evil, whose stems are in thy acts." (Ibid., IX.28)

Here (i) 'celebration' means the recitation of His names, and (ii) striving for the sake of devotion, although it is a common thing in life, is mentioned here, as the topic is the declaration of the subsidiaries to devotion. (iii) Firmness in vow consists in the observance of fast on the eleventh day of the moon, etc., in a spirit of devotion. (iv) Bowing is the operation of the raising of the hands to the head, etc., in token of self-abasement, and (v) the sacrifice of knowledge is twofold: distinguished as the superior and the inferior according as it has the unity or the plurality as its object. (vi) Thinking on nought besides is the contemplation and constant remembrance of Him alone. (vii) Sacrifice is worship; so is also (viii) the offering of a leaf, etc., in the name of the Lord. (ix) The giving over of all is the giving over of all actions prescribed and prohibited to this Supreme Lord.

Not only are these the only subsidiaries, but those other observances which are contained in such revelations about service or adoration as "Let one serve Manas as Brahman" (*Chāndogya Upaniṣad,* III.xviii.1), "Among the Ādityas I am Viṣṇu" (*Gītā,* X.21), etc., are also the subsidiaries of devotion. If you ask, why? We reply, because even the entire Brahmakāṇḍa of the Veda is declaratory of devotion and its means.—3

ताभ्यः पावित्र्युपक्रमात् ।। २ । २ । ४ ।।

ताभ्यः (*tābhyaḥ*), by these. पावित्र्यम् (*pāvitryam*), purity. उपक्रमात् (*upakramāt*), from the introduction.

4. By the secondary forms of devotion purity is produced, as is seen from the introduction.—59

"By these" i.e., by the secondary form of devotion, is produced "purity," i.e., the destruction of sins which are the cause of the impurity of the internal organ. This destruction it is which is the doorway to the higher devotion. How? because they are declared after introducing the subject by the words "this is purifying, excellent" (*Gītā,* IX.2); because devotion is an attribute of the internal organ; because purity is an intimate and not an extraneous means of devotion.—4

तासु प्रधानयोगात् फलाधिक्यमेके ।। २ । २ । ५ ।।

तासु (*tāsu*), in them. प्रधानयोगात् (*pradhāna-yogāt*), from the conjunction of the principal, i.e., the higher devotion. फलाधिक्यम् (*phala-ādhikyam*), excess of fruit, एके (*eke*), some.

5. Some infer an excess of fruit from the conjunction of the principal with these.—60

Some teachers consider that when the subsidiary character of these very practices, e.g., celebration of His names, etc., is established from the context, etc., is such texts as "Whoever offers to me with devotion" (*Gītā,* IX.26), "Bowing to me with devotion", etc., the additional mention of the conjunction of devotion therein is intended to imply an excess of fruit in the performance of these practices by those in whom devotion has been aroused.—5

नाम्नेति जैमिनिः सम्भवात् ।। २ । २ । ६ ।।

नाम्ना (*nāmnā*), as a name. इति (*iti*), thus. जैमिनि: (*jaiminiḥ*), the sage of that name. सम्भवात् (*sambhavāt*), from possibility.

6. Jaimini interprets it as a name, from the possibility (of the co-existence of the fruit and the employment of the means in the same subject).—61

The teacher Jaimini considers that, their subsidiary character having been established, since, as in the case of "Let one who is using a spell against an enemy sacrifice with the *śyena*" (*Āśvalāyana Śrautasūtra,* IX.vii), etc., there is the possibility of explanation in the sense of co-existence (of the act and the end) in one and the same subject, in this way "Let one accomplish the higher devotion by the celebration of His names with devotion, by giving with devotion", etc., the word, devotion, is intended otherwise, i.e., as a name, and is not intended to imply a different fruit, as such an interpretation would violate the law of parsimony.—6

अत्राङ्गप्रयोगानां यथाकालसम्भवो गृहादिवत् ।। २ । २ । ७ ।।

अत्र (*atra*), here. अङ्गप्रयोगानां (*aṅga-prayogānām*) of the employment of the subsidiaries. यथाकालसम्भव: (*yathā-kāla-sambhavaḥ*), according to time and necessity. गृहादिवत् (*gṛha-ādi-vat*), as in the case of a house, etc.

7. Here the employment of these subsidiaries is to be according to time and necessity.—62

There are three alternatives, viz., the performance of the celebration of His names, bowing to Him, etc., may be simultaneous, or it may be of any one of them singly, or it may be of all of them one after another. Of these, in the first alternative, the non-performance of even any one of them would entail the failure of all the rest; in the second, it would be a law of nature that a diversity of causes produced one and the same effect; while the third is contrary to the meaning of the text, and would also on the ground of redundancy entail the non-performance of the others after one was performed and the higher devotion was produced thereby. Therefore these different subsidiaries would be the cause of mutual opposition and futility. Such is the *prima facie* conclusion (*Pūrvapakṣa*).

But the (*siddhānta*) established truth is that all of them without exception are the means (towards the higher devotion), as there exists the evidence that such is the case; while there exists no evidence to prove the necessity for their simultaneous performance. There should be simultaneous performance of only those, of which, e.g., perfume, flower, incense, lamps, oblations, etc., the simultaneous use is enjoined in the *śāstras*. But of the others the performance is to be according to time and according to necessity, as in the building of a house, etc.; i.e., just as the collection of the materials for a house such as thatching grass, posts, etc., is made sometimes all at once and sometimes in succession; and it does not follow from this circumstance alone that the thatching grass, etc., are not the material causes of a house. It follows therefore that the production of the higher devotion takes place through all the subsidiary means when they have shown their respective efficacy by causing the destruction of such sins as they are severally competent to destroy. And so it is declared (*Gītā*, VII.19):

"At the end of many births, he who has knowledge attains Me."—7

ईश्वरतुष्टेरेकोऽपि बली।।२।२।८।।

ईश्वरतुष्टेः (*īśvara-tuṣṭeḥ*), from the pleasing of the Lord. एकः (*ekaḥ*), a single one. अपि (*api*), even. बली (*balī*), strong.

8. Through the pleasing of the Lord, even one, being strong, may be effectual.—63

Among these subsidiaries, whichever one becomes strong by exceeding performance, that, even though single, prevails towards the evolution of the higher devotion by producing the pleasure of the Supreme Lord. Just as an earthly lord is not pleased even by the careless services of a number of servants, but is pleased by even a single servant by whom the act of the shampooing of his feet is performed regularly with hearty zeal; so is it here.

Even by any one or other of the subsidiaries, celebration of His names, etc., resolutely practised, devotion is attained, through the favour of the Lord; as it is declared, for instance:

"Taking up the practice of knowledge, get thy mind always fixed on Me;
Having thy mind fixed on Me, all difficulties, through My favour, shalt thou cross over." (*Gītā*, XVIII.57-58)

Likewise such special strength may be caused in someone of the means by a certain time, etc. As for instance:

"By meditation in the Kṛta, by performing sacrifices in the Tretā, by worship in the Dvāpara,
What one obtains, that one obtains in the Kali by celebrating Keśava is song." (*Brahma Purāṇa*, XCVII.166)

Nor need any confusion of effects be apprehended, because the celebration of His names and the other means are individually as such the means towards the evolution of the devotion to be produced by each of them singly when it is strong.—8

If you ask, does everyone of the subsidiaries included in the celebration of His names, etc., need purity (vide aphorism 59) as the doorway through which to cause the appearance of the higher devotion, or do any of them have any other doorway? The author replies:

अबन्धोऽर्पणस्य मुखम् ।। २ । २ । ६ ।।

अबन्धः (*a-bandhaḥ*), non-existence of bondage. अर्पणस्य (*arpaṇasya*), of surrender of all actions to him. मुखम् (*mukham*), entrance.

9. The non-existence of bondage as the result of the surrender of all actions to Him is the only entrance.—64

The only entrance for the appearance of devotion is the non-existence of bondage consisting in the non-production of their respective fruits (i.e., merits and demerits) by actions, good and evil, which have been surrendered to the Lord. As it is declared:

"Thus shalt thou be delivered from the fruit, good and evil, whose stems are in thy acts." (*Gītā,* IX.28)

The formula for this surrender of actions is also found in another Purāṇa:

"Voluntarily or even involuntarily, whatever I do, good or evil,
All that is surrendered to Thee; I do it as impelled by Thee."

Nor would such surrender entail a man's acting as he pleased without any risk of consequences; because by virtue of his acting under His impulsion the absence of sinful conduct also should form a subsidiary to the act of surrender; as says the Smṛti: "Relying on the support of the Veda, let no one be attached to sinful acts." Therefore, purity must have something other than purity of action as the object of its reference.

Here by good action is to be understood such action as is prescribed for one's particular stage of life for daily or for occasional performance. From the thorough observance of the stages of life, result such fruits as the world of Brahmā, etc., on the attainment of which delay takes place in obtaining *mukti;* such as these are therefore "bondage". But when surrendered to Brahman, they do not, as is well-known, produce their fruits. Similarly, in the case also of optional acts and sinful acts performed whether volunarily or in ignorance, there is the same non-existence of fruit when they are afterwards surrendered to Him.—9

Now, among the secondary forms of devotion themselves, their individual distinctions are going to be considered. Therein, as regards meditation or contemplation (vide aphorism 58), is it to be restricted only to those of the characteristic forms of the object of devotion such as are described in the Śruti and the Smṛti, as for instance:

"That golden *Puruṣa* who is seen in the sun, with golden beard and with golden hair, etc." (*Chāndogya Upaniṣad,* I.vi.6). And likewise:

"Ever is to be meditated on as residing in the centre of the orb of the sun,
Nārāyaṇa, seated on a lotus seat,
Wearing bracelets and *makara* earrings bearing a crest,
Decked with a string of pearls round the neck, having a form of gold,
and holding a conch and discus." (*Nārada Pañcarātra,* XI.71)

Or is it to be restricted to the full manifestations, etc., of the Supreme as revealed elsewhere? Here as a limitation of meditation *prima facie* is suggested through the revelation of the special forms of the object of meditation, it is declared by the author:

ध्याननियमस्तु दृष्टसौकर्यात् ।। २ । २ । १० ।।

ध्याननियमः (*dhyāna-niyamaḥ*), limitation of meditation. तु (*tu*), but. दृष्टसौकर्यात् (*dṛṣṭa-saukaryāt*), on account of the facility of the performance of meditation on a form which has been seen.

10. But the limitation of meditation is on account of the facility of its performance on a form which has been seen.—65

The declaration of the limitation of meditation as regards the forms to be meditated on his as its object such forms as have been seen; because were the objects manifold, distraction of mind would be possible. Therefore it is to be known that the declaration of limitation is merely for the sake of facility; as, if the objects of meditation were such forms as had not been seen, there might arise the risk of an option and other distractions. It follows therefore that meditation may have as its object all manifestations of the Lord, partial, full, or formless, according as these have been revealed. Hence it is that the milkmaids as well as Śiśupāla and others attained the fruit which is hard to attain by meditation, even without observing the above limitation of meditation (i.e., even without meditating on the forms of the Lord as described in the Śruti and the Smṛti).—10

तद्यजिः पूजायामितरेषां नैवम् ।। २ । २ । ११ ।।

तद्यजिः (*tat-yajiḥ*), that *yaj*—to sacrifice. पूजायाम (*pūjāyām*), in worship. इतरेषां (*itareṣām*), of the other sacrifices. न (*na*), not. एवम् (*evam*), so.

11. The root *yaj*—to sacrifice there is in the sense of worship; (because its sole reference is the Lord; this is) not so in the case of the other sacrifices.—66

The doubt is whether the verb *yaj*—to sacrifice used in "those who sacrifice to Me, go to Me also" (*Gītā,* IX.35) has reference to such sacrifices as the well-known *jyotiṣṭoma,* etc., or whether it denotes worship. In regard to this doubt we say that this verb *yaj*—to sacrifice has been used in the sense of worship alone. How is this know? you ask. We reply that by the injunction "Let one worship Viṣṇu", etc., daily and optional worship has been prescribed in which the object of worship as expressly declared is Viṣṇu; and that in the text of the *Gītā* under consideration all that is enjoined is merely that the worship so prescribed is a subsidiary means of the higher devotion, and not that in this worship the object of worship is Viṣṇu. In the case of the other sacrifices, on the other hand, it is nowhere revealed that they are performed in reference to the Lord. If then they were to be denoted by the verb *yaj*—to sacrifice in the text of the *Gītā* we are discussing, we would have to supply both that they were performed in reference to the Lord and also that they had connection with devotion; in which case the text would have spoken in two sentences instead of one as it has done.

Now, if you say that there may be some connection with devotion of the sacrifice which is enjoined in "To Viṣṇu Urukrama he brings forth progeny or an oblation of milk and butter", etc., (because the word Viṣṇu is expressly mentioned there), we reply, that is so, because optional acts (undertaken with a particular end in view, as in this case, for the birth of a child) are by their fruits themselves rendered free from desire; while in the case of a daily worship the occasion or reason for the performance of which is the preservation of life, there is no bar to the existence of connection with devotion therein, and it requires no stretch of imagination to see that the presence of this connection is continual, since the worship is obligatory for daily performance. Hence in the censure in the Mokṣa Dharma section of the *Mahābhārata* of acts of merit attended with injury to living beings, it it declared:

"The righteous minded Manu declared avoidance of injury in all acts.

Men affected by desires slaughter animals on the outer altar. Those who know Viṣṇu sacrifice only in the right way, with puddings and flowers. Such is also the sacrifice recollected in the Smṛti."

(Śānti Parva, CCLXV.6870)—11

Now follow three *adhikaraṇas* or sections on the subject of worship.

पादोदकं तु पाद्यमव्याप्तेः ।। २ । २ । १२ ।।

पादोदकं (*pāda-udakam*), water of His feet. तु (*tu*), but. पाद्यम् (*pādyam*), water for washing the feet. अव्याप्तेः (*a-vyāpteḥ*), on account of non-application to all cases.

12. But "water of (His) feet" is water for washing the feet, as otherwise it would not apply to all cases where it ought to apply.—67

Thus is it recollected (in *Nṛsiṃha Purāṇa,* LIX.46):

"Of the Gaṅgā, Prayāga, Gayā, Puṣkara, and Naimiṣa,
Those sacred waters of Kurujāṅgala and the Yamunā,
The waters of holy places sanctify sinners after a lapse of time,
The water of the Lord's feet purifies immediately."

Now, here does the phrase "water of the (Lord's) feet" means water connected with the feet or does it mean water first poured on the feet and then dropped therefrom? Such being the doubt, we say that "water of the feet" means nothing more than water for washing the feet. How is this known? you ask. We reply that otherwise the phrase would not be applicable to some cases which ought to be included. For, thus, direct connection of the Lord's feet with water is not possible; nor even through the incarnation, because in the case of incarnation also it is impossible that this should be always in the presence of the performer of the ceremony. But through connection of the water with the feet of the image which is the immediate basis of the worship, there might be, you may say, a transference of that connection to the Lord's feet; we point out that even in that case, there could be no such transference, inasmuch as images both consecrated and unconsecrated are invoked for the purpose of worship, and further in such cases of worship as the Śāligrāma Ammonites, etc., there is a total absence of feet. Regard being had to the application of the phrase to these cases, let it mean simply water for washing the feet, as otherwise you will have to imagine very remote connections such as, e.g., through the image, etc.—12

स्वयमर्पितं ग्राह्यमविशेषात्।।२।२।१३।।

स्वयम् (*svayam*), himself. अर्पितं (*arpitaṃ*), offered. ग्राह्यम् (*grāhyam*), may be taken. अविशेषात् (*a-viśeṣāt*), from absence of distintion.

13. What is offered (by the worshipper) himself may be taken (by him); as there is no distinction (intended between worshippers in general and the Sātvatas).—68

What is offered to the Lord at a worship, e.g., eatables, garlands, etc., is ordained as having to be finally disposed of by distribution among the votaries, etc., by such texts as "Viṣṇu-offerings to the Sātvatas". Now here from the very fact that to be a Sātvata (i.e., prince of the Sātvata clan) is not intended to be a special qualification, the offerings can be taken also by the devotee of the Lord himself, i.e., can be appropriated to his own use by eating, wearing, etc. Such is the meaning. The injunction about the final disposal of the offerings is fulfilled even if the worshipper takes them himself. But trickery in religious matters is certainly to be avoided. Just as even of the cake offered in reference to Agni, etc., there is a final disposal according to the latter part of the *mantra* "He puts the offering to Agni Sviṣṭakṛt from the upper half; the four priests, with the institutor as the fifth, eat the cake" (*Āpastamba Śrautasūtra,* III.i.2), so also is the final disposal under consideration quite in accordance with the injunction. Otherwise, one could not finally make over the offerings even to the Sātvatas; as they are properly belonging to another. If you say that one can give them to the Sātvatas from the injunction; we reply, No, for the exclusion of one's self is not declared in the injunction (so that if one could give them to the Sātvatas one could also take them for one's self, but to this you object). If you rejoin that there is the exclusion of one's self, as otherwise injunctions such as "Let one give to the Brāhmaṇas," etc., would entail giving to one's self also from one's being a Brāhmaṇa; we reply, no, because the giving consists in the transference of the right of ownership to another by the destruction of one's own rights of ownership in the thing given. Nor is such exclusion of one's self appropriate in the final disposed of the offering at the close of a ceremony. From seeing the final disposal of even the cake to the performer of the ceremony, we infer that, like purchase, the final disposal also truly is a means of transferring ownership. So then where there is an absence of any other Sātvata or devotee, there the futility of the injunction is certainly to be avoided even by the performer himself taking the offerings. Similarly is the injunction to be understood also in regard to keeping the water for washing the feet, etc., offered by himself. Moreover, the declaration "He is a thief indeed who enjoys objects given by the gods, not having offered these to them" (*Gītā*, III.12) is in our favour, as it clearly implies the enjoyment of things previously offered to the gods. Here the agent being the same in the two clauses, it is perceived that the object also must be the same, when the ownership implied in the one clause is lost by the act of giving implied in the other clause, since action denoted by the negative prefix 'not' accompanied by the infinite verbal termination 'ing'; in *a-pradāya,* not having offered, must have syntactical connection with the action denotec' by "enjoys" by way of co-existence in the sme subject; as there is no evidence to show that the things mentioned by "objects given by the gods" are other things of the same kind as those mentioned in the remainder of the sentence. Therefore it is to be considered that even offerings made to the gods may be enjoyed by the offerer in the absence of any hindrance.—13

निमित्तगुणव्यपेक्षणादपराधेषु व्यवस्था।।२।२।१४।।

निमित्तगुणव्यपेक्षणात् (*nimitta-guṇa-vyapekṣaṇāt*), from reference to the occasion and nature. अपराधेषु (*aparādheṣu*), in the case of failings, faults, offences. व्यवस्था (*vyavasthā*), regulation.

14. The regulation in the case of 'failings' is with reference to their occasion and nature.—69

After introducing the subject with the words "Those failings in the worship of the gods are enumerated to be thirty-two" (*Varāha Purāṇa,* CXXIV.4), the thirty-two failings and their several expiations are laid down. Here the doubt arises whether the abandonment of all failings is a part of the worship, or whether the abandonment of some of them is a part of the worship, and of some of them an end in itself. In regard to this doubt it is declared—

"Whatever man worships Me with a flower unfit for use in worship,
His fall I declare, which hear thou, O Vasundharā."

(*Varāha Purāṇa,* CXXIV.65)

Here flowers unfit for use having been thrown overboard, they are not a subsidiary means of worship. But, when they are offered by mistake, etc., in going through the course of the worship, there is an expiation which has reference to that occasion. Where, again, one commits the failing of breaking the course of the worship according to the declaration, "Who offers incense to Me, not having offered perfume and garlands" (*Varāha Purāṇa,* XXV.36), as the course prescribed in the case of each worship is a part of the worship, it is to be considered that the expiation thereof is a part of the worship, because there is thereby the removal of the worship's being defective in a part. Where it is heard, without the mention of worship, "But whoever approaches Me, not having chewed the stick with which to brush the teeth" (*Varāha Purāṇa,* CXXVI.1), there it is manifest indeed that the avoidance of the failing is an end in itself. Such is then the regulation in regard to expiations.—14

Thus the connection of worship with devotion being established, the author declares that "A leaf, a flower, a fruit, a handful of water" (*Gītā,* IX.26) it is laid down that every offering intended for the Lord is a subsidiary means of devotion.

पत्रादेर्दानमन्यथा हि वैशिष्ट्यम् ।। २ । २ । १५ ।।

पत्रादेः (*patra-ādeḥ*), of a leaf, etc. दानम् (*dānam*), offering. अन्यथा (*anyathā*), otherwise. हि (*hi*), for. वैशिष्ट्यम् (*vaiśiṣṭyam*), qualifiedness.

15. The offering of a leaf and of all else (is meant in the above text of the *Gītā*); for, otherwise, the offering mentioned by it would be qualified.—70

The injunction in the *Gītā* that they are the subsidiaries of devotion is not confined to the offerings of the four articles mentioned therein, but applies to all offerings intended for the Lord which have been declared by such texts as:

"Whatever is most desired in the world, whatever else is loved at home,
That is all to be given to the discus-holding god of gods, to please Him."
(Cowell)

Otherwise the offering mentioned in the *Gītā* would mean only the offering which contained the four things, namely a leaf, etc. In that case, as the injunction would imply the offering of each of the four things separately, the sentence, instead of being one, should have been split into four. Therefore it is proper to hold this view only of the text that by the declaration of "A leaf, etc.", it re-enforces the offering elsewhere laid down, and then enjoins its being a subsidiary of devotion, just as by the text "He wears the sacred thread over the left shoulder" (*Taittirīya Saṃhitā,* II.v.11) the obligatory duty of wearing the sacred thread over the left shoulder is enjoined as a subsidiary of the *darśa* sacrifice.—15

सुकृतजत्वात् परहेतुभावाच्च क्रियासु श्रेयस्यः ।। २ । २ । १६ ।।

सुकृतजत्वात् (*sukṛta-ja-tvāt*), from being produced from good works.

परहेतुभावात् *para-hetu-bhāvāt,* from being the cause of the higher devotion. च (*ca*), and. क्रियासु (*kriyāsu*), among acts. श्रेयस्यः (*śreyasyaḥ*), superior.

16. (These secondary forms of devotion are) superior to all other acts, because they are produced from good works, because they are the causes of the higher devotion.—71

These forms of devotion are really superior to all other acts; how?—because they are the causes of the higher devotion, and because they are produced from other meritorious acts. For example:

"Many, being purified by knowledge and penance, have attained to devotion (*bhāva*) to Me.
Whoso in what manner approach Me, in the same manner do I attach Myself to them." (*Gītā,* IV.10-11)

The word *bhāva* also is applied to devotion; as, e.g., in:

"Do not fishes dwell in the water of the Gaṅgā?
Do not birds dwell in temples?
Being destitute of *bhāva* (devotion) they do not get the fruit,
From dwelling in the watering place and in the sacred temple."

Similarly:

"Four types of men, all having done good works, worship Me, O Arjuna." (*Gītā,* VII.16)

Here (it is declared that) as the secondary forms of devotion are produced from previous good works, they are superior to these.

The present aphorism (therefore) declares that the discussion is rightly directed to a Mīmāṃsā of Devotion rather than to a Mīmāṃsā of *karma.*—16

But, you may say, among the devotees the relation of the higher and the lower does not exist; if it existed, why is mention made of the four classes as all standing on the same level? in:

"Four types of men, all having done good works, worship Me, O Arjuna:
The afflicted, the inquisitive, the entreative, and the wise, O chief of the Bharatas." (*Gītā,* VII.16)

To this the author replies:

गौणं त्रैविध्यमितरेण स्तुत्यर्थत्वात् साहचर्यम्।।२।२।१७।।

गौणं (*gauṇaṃ*), secondary. त्रैविध्यम् (*traividhyam*), threefoldness. इतरेण (*itareṇa*), with the other. स्तुत्यर्थत्वात् (*stuti-artha-tvāt*), having praise for its purpose. साहचर्यम् (*sāhacaryam*), association.

17. The three are secondary; their association with the other, (i.e., the primary) is for the sake of doing them honour.—72

The secondary are the three only, (viz., the devotion of the afflicted, the inquisitive, and the entreative). But the Śruti's associating them with the principal one (in the above *Gītā* text) is for the purpose of giving them honour, just as is the mention of the ministers in conjunction with the king.

And thus the devotion of the afflicted consists in remembering the Lord, celebrating His names, etc., for the sake of the destruction of sin, deliverance from calamity, etc. The devotion of the inquisitive consists in such practices as are performed for the sake of knowledge. And again, for example:

"Him, this Self, the Brāhmaṇa desire to know by studying the Veda, by sacrifice, by gift, by penance, by fast."

(*Bṛhadāraṇyaka Upaniṣad,* VI.iv.22)

Similarly:

"Having worshipped Him by their respective works, men attain perfection. (*Gītā,* XVIII.48)

"Who deviates not from the duties of his caste,
Who has equal regard for self, friend, and adversary,
Who steals not, smites none down,
Know him, steady in mind, to be the devotee of Viṣṇu."

(*Viṣṇu Purāṇa,* III.vii.16)

—according to such texts the devotion called the desire for knowledge consists in the performance, for the sake of knowledge, of such acts as the studying of the Veda, etc., prescribed for the respective caste and stage of life of the devotee. (Thus the devotion of the inquisitive is twofold). The devotion called the entreaty for objects of desire is also of two kinds. Of these the one which is cultivated for the sake of the higher devotion has been described before; the other which is cultivated for the sake of kingdom, heaven, etc., is in the form of the celebration of His names, etc. For example:

"Lovely terrestrial objects of desire,—a supreme state to be praised by the denizens of heaven,

Also *nirvāṇa* excellent does a man obtain, when Viṣṇu is worshipped by him." (*Viṣṇu Purāṇa,* III.vii.3)

Here the attainment of *nirvāṇa* is by means of the higher devotion; hence the entreativeness lies in the desire for the higher devotion; because the text conveys the same import, as "And who worship Me, with devotion, they are in Me, and I in them also." (*Gītā,* IX.19)

And what is declared in the *Bhāgavata* (VII.v.22-23):

"Hearing, celebrating, remembering Viṣṇu, serving his feet,
Worshipping, praising, serving, befriending, consecrating one's self,
If this ninefold devotion is yielded by a man to Viṣṇu."

all that is to be appropriately distributed among those very (four) divisions of ours. Even though there is thus a plurality of subjects to which these adjective coremonials are (simultaneously) distributed, this is no fault.—17

But it may be asked, when the celebration of His names, etc., have been declared as being the subsidiaries (of the higher devotion in aphorism 58), how can the character of being the principal belong to them in the case of the devotions called affliction, etc.? Such an enquiry being possible, the author declares:

वहिरन्तरस्थमुभयमवेष्टिसववत् ।। २।२।१८।।

वहिरन्तरस्थम् (*vahir-antara-stham*), standing outside as well as inside. उभयम् (*ubhayam*), both. अवेष्टिसववत् (*aveṣṭi-sava-vat*), like the *aveṣṭi* ceremony and the Bṛihaspati offering in the sacrifice, *vājapeya*.

18. (The celebration of His names, etc.) are both outside and inside (the higher devotion), as is the case with the *aveṣṭi* and the Bṛhaspati offering.—73

The celebration of His names, etc., being subsidiaries of the higher devotion, are inside it. They also excel in being outside it, since the Śruti declares that they produce other fruits without being practised as subsidiaries of the higher devotion. Just as the *aveṣṭi* ceremony included in the *rājasūya* sacrifice excels in itself becoming the principal through connection with other fruits without being performed as a subsidiary of the *rājasūya,* or just as again the Bṛhaspati offering, although it is sometimes the principal, is a subsidiary of the *vājapeya* sacrifice, so is it here also, according as the distinction is rendered necessary by the existence or non-existence of sufficient reason for it. Similarly, according to the declaration:

"Through inattentiveness of the performers of some rite, if anything fails in sacrifices,

Through the remembering of Viṣṇu alone that will be complete, so says the Śruti."

the remembrance of Viṣṇu (for example) can be practised as an occasional subsidiary of all acts; hence it is a subsidiary by nature. And this subsidiary character is not opposed to its being the principal is relation to the fruit of heaven, etc. (which it is also competent to produce).—18

Some special feature of the devotion of the afflicted is now considered.

स्मृतिकीर्त्योः कथादेश्चार्त्तौ प्रायश्चित्तभावात् ।। २ । २ । १९ ।।

स्मृतिकीर्त्योः (*smṛti-kīrttyoḥ*), of the remembrance of the Lord and the celebration of His names. कथादेः (*katha-ādeḥ*), of discourses about Him, etc. च (*ca*), and. आर्त्तौ (*ārttau*), in the devotioin of the afflicted. प्रायश्चित्तभावात् (*prāyaś-citta-bhāvāt*), being of the nature of expiation.

19. (The inclusion) of the remembrance of the Lord and the celebration of His names and of discourses about Him, etc., in the devotion of the afflicted is on account of their being of the nature of expiation.—74

The inclusion of the remembrance of the Lord, the celebration of His names, discourses about Him, bowing to Him, etc., in the devotion of the afflicted is made, because they are declared to be the causes of the abolition of such and such sins to those suffering the afflictions of hell produced by those sins. For example:

"Severe in the case of serious sins, light also in the case of light sins,
Expiations, O Maitreya, have been declared by Manu and others.
Expiations infinite, whether penances, good works, or the like,
Whatever they be, superior to them all is the constant remembrance of Krṣna." (*Viṣṇu Purāṇa,* II.vi.32, 33)

Again:

"The celebration of whose names, with devotion, is the excellent consumer,
O Maitreya, of all sins, as fire is of metals." (*Viṣṇu Purāṇa,* I.vii.9)

Similarly:

"The observance of all the stages of life, bathing in all holy waters,
Is not so fruitful, O Sauti, as is the discourse about Nārāyaṇa.

Purified in body have we become by hearing this discourse from the beginning,
Whose subject is Nārāyaṇa, which confers merit, and abolishes all sins."
(*Mahābhārata,* Śānti Parva, Mokṣa Dharma, CCCXLV.13305-6)

Therefore their inclusion in the devotion of "affliction" is quite right.—19

भूयसामनुष्ठितिरिति चेदाप्रयाणमुपसंहारान्महत्स्वपि ।।

भूयसाम् (*bhūyasām*), of the more severe expiations. अननुष्ठितिः (*an-anuṣṭhitiḥ*), non-performance. इति (*iti*), thus. चेत् (*cet*), if. आप्रयाणम् (*ā-prayāṇam*), till the passing away. उपसंहारात् (*upasaṃhārāt*), from ending. महत्सु (*mahatsu*), in the case of more serious sins. अपि (*api*), also.

20. If (you say that this would imply) the non-performance of the more severe expiations, (we reply, no), because from their (i.e. of the supposed lighter expiations, e.g., the remembrance of the Lord, etc.) ending at death, they are efficacious in the case of the more serious sins also, or they are included among the more severe expiations also.—75

You may say, "So be it; since the opposite would be contrary to reason, it is proper to hold that the above declarations must have reference to very light sins only; otherwise all those expiations which involved considerable hardship in their performance would not be performed and would so far have become unauthoritative." We reply that such is not the case; since in the acts included in the devotion of the afflicted there is also an excess of hardship, inasmuch as the Smṛti enjoins their (continuance till and) conclusion at death. For example:

"Therefore, day and night, remembering Viṣṇu, a man, O Muni,
Does not go to hell, being purified and having all his sins destroyed."
(*Viṣṇu Purāṇa,* II.vi.29)

According to this declaration the conclusion of the practice of the means (i.e., remembering the Lord, etc.) is to take place at death in unbroken continuity with its commencement, since the commencement and the conclusion must have the same sense (and therefore as no particular time is fixed in the above text for the commencement of the practice, so no particular time can be fixed for its conclusion). Such is the import. Nor is any time specified for the commencement, whereby, from the contradiction to that, the conclusion could have a different sense also (and refer to any particular time). And thus, as all are alike in point of hardship, unauthoritativeness in the shape of non-performance does not, as supposed, attach to the other expiations.

"At morning, at night, so at sunset, noon, etc., remembering" (*Viṣṇu Purāṇa,* II.vi.35) which divides the practice of the means into certain periods, is nothing but a repetition (*anuvāda**). Nor again does this belong to a section of the Smṛti dealing with one who is repentant as its subject-matter. Since the (preceding) declaration:

> "Sin having been committed, in whomsoever man repentance arises
> His best expiation is the one remembrance of Hari."
>
> (*Viṣṇu Purāṇa,* II.vi.34)

also is a repetition (*anuvāda*) of that repentance which is a subsidiary of all expiations, the declaration contains a repetition also of that 'one' expiation which is independent of the other expiations and which logically follows from the context. Otherwise, the sentences would be different, and would have each a specified subject-matter of its own.** Therefore, the preceding declarations (*Viṣṇu Purāṇa,* II.vi.32, 33 ff.) are not *arthavādas* or recommendations, inasmuch as they are comprehended within the reference of the relative pronoun 'which' and are accordingly repetitions (*anuvāda*) of the several injunctions to which they are respectively appropriate. Hence it is that elsewhere also the continuity of the practice of the means has been declared by such declarations as:

> "The emissaries, (of Yama), their staves and fetters, nor Yama, nor
> again the torments of hell,

*"The *arthaveda* is properly a persuasive enforcement of a previous injunction; it gives the purpose of the injunction, and illustrates its power by positive or negative examples. Thus there is an *arthaveda* for the *sarvajit* sacrifice (*Tāṇḍya Br.*, XVI.7, 2): "Verily by the *sarvajit* the gods conquered all, it is for the attainment of all, for the conquest of all; by this a man attains all, conquers all." The *anuvāda* is the reiteration or re-inculcation of an injunction it may be with further details, but without dwelling on the purpose of the injunction itself. Thus, after the injunction 'he is to offer the *agnihotra*', we have an *anuvāda* 'he offers it with curds' (this is a *guṇānuvāda*); or, again we have an injunction 'let him who desires prosperity offer a white goat to Vāyu' followed by the *anuvāda* 'the wind (Vāyu) is the swiftest of gods' (*Taitt. Saṃh.*, III.4, 3), this is a *stutyarthānuvāda*."—Cowell

**"i.e. the first part clearly declares what had been already enjoined (i.e., that repentance is necessary in every expiation), and it is therefore an *anuvāda;* and the second part must also be an *anuvāda,* unless we are to suppose that the two parts of the sentence (although connected by *yat* and *tat*) are different, the one being an *anuvāda* or simple reiteration and the other an *arthavāda.*"—Cowell

Have power against him whose soul is always dependent on Keśava.
The names of the discus-armed let him celebrate at all times, in all places;
No impurity belongs to him, as He is the purifier."

(*Viṣṇu Purāṇa,* III.vii.34, 35)—20

लघ्वपि भक्ताधिकारे महत्क्षेपकमपरसर्वहानात् ।। २ । २ । २१ ।।

लघु (*laghu*), a little, trifling. अपि (*api*), even. भक्ताधिकारे (*bhakta-adhikāre*), in the case of the devotees, where devotees are concerned. महत्क्षेपकम् (*mahat-kṣepakam*), destructive of great sins. अपरसर्वहानात् (*apara-sarva-hānāt*), from thee abolition of everything else.

21. Even though it is trifling, it is sufficient to overthrow great sins, where devotees are concerned, since there is therefrom the abolition of all other expiations.—76

Even though trifling, the remembrance of the Lord, the celebration of His names, etc. (practised) for once only, become the overthrowers, i.e., the destroyers, of even great sins; since thence there is the cognition of the abolition characterised as abandonment of all the other expiations, where the devotees are concerned. Such is the meaning. As it has been sung:

"Abandoning all duties, fly to Me as thy one refuge;
I will deliver thee from all sins, grieve not." (*Gītā,* XVIII.66)

For here the meaning is not that the flying to the Lord is to be preceded by the abandonment of acts which are 'optional'* and in which one may engage from desire; because, as there is no sin in the abandonment of 'optional acts, what is to be removed by the Lord? Now, if you say that there may be a different sin which is to be destroyed; we demur, as the supposition would entail that the abandonment of 'optional' acts would have the object called *adṛṣṭa* (demerit, lit., unseen) as its fruit (whereas the

*"Ceremonial works are of three kinds, 'constant', 'occasional' and 'voluntary'. The 'constant' are those continually enjoined through a Brahman's (*sic* a twiceborn's) life, as the daily and fortnightly offerings: the 'occasional' are enjoined on certain occasions, as recovery from sickness, an eclipse, etc., the 'voluntary' are directed to some special end, as 'let him who desires heaven offer the *jyotiṣṭoma*'. It is generally held that the first two are positive duties and cannot be omitted without sin; but their performance does not produce bondage by causing merit in the offerer. The 'voluntary' offerings necessitate a future reward, and as they thus produce bondage, they should be avoided by the devotee. Śāṇḍilya, however holds that even 'constant' and 'occasional' works, as well as 'voluntary', produce 'merit', and so tend to cause bondage, unless they are surrendered in faith to *Īśvara*."—Cowell on aphorism 64

very nature of an 'optional' act is that it is such as one need not perform unless one desires the particular fruit which it is to produce; so that the fruit of such an act cannot be *adṛṣṭa* (lit. unseen, merit) but is always one which is previously known.

Nor is its meaning that the flying to the Lord is to be preceded by the abandonment of even 'daily' and 'occasional' acts; for, if there is any positive injunction in favour of their abandonment, no sin accrues therefrom; what is to be removed? Now, if you say that there is no such injunction; we reply, do not say so, as the very declaration of the *Gītā* and the like contains such an injunction, and consequently the act (i.e., abandonment) so enjoined cannot produce any sin.

If you say that after describing the *saṃnyāsin* (ascetic) by *anuvāda* by the phrase "abandoning all duties", the declaration of the *Gītā* has reference to him as its object; we reply, no, for, the Smṛti lays down expiations, etc., for the *saṃnyāsins,* such as that in the case of their breaking the vow by connection with women, etc., and as consequently there would arise the possibility of the alternative performance of the remembrance of the Lord and the other subsidiaries of devotion, or of the expiations, etc., prescribed, there would also arise the possibility of the non-performance of the more severe expiations as you feared before (vide aphorism 75). Nor can this defect be avoided by assuming the unbroken continuity of the practice of the acts of remembrance, etc., because even a trifling practice (e.g., one remembrance) is capable of destroying great sins (in this case also), according to such declarations as:

"Even though filled with a great sin, if he meditates on Viṣṇu for the twinkling of an eye,
The ascetic becomes again the purifier even of those who purify the company in which they dwell." (Cowell)

Moreover, by reason of its being nowhere near (in the context), the stage of life called *saṃnyāsa* or renunciation of the world, ought not to enter the mind at all (in the present discussion). Therefore, just as in the world when one says to another "Leaving all others, have faith in me, I will destroy all your troubles", the abandonment of other means of destroying troubles is understood; so from the declaration itself quoted above the abandonment of other means of destroying internal sins is understood.

Although this declaration which to a certain extent enjoins *saṃnyāsa* or the renunciation of the world is read in the same chapter, the chapter as a whole has not *saṃnyāsa* as its subject-matter, because the general subject (*prakaraṇa*) and the context (*sannidhāna*) are of superior force in determining the sense. Moreover, in this chapter, by such passages as:

"The surrender of optional acts the seers know to be *saṃnyāsa*."
(*Gītā,* XVIII.2)

it is the abandonment of optional acts that has been declared, and not the stage or order of life called *saṃnyāsa.* Likewise the single remembrance, etc., have as their only object of reference that person who, along with the resolution to abandon all other expiations, desires to pass over affliction solely by means of the Lord's names, etc.

And thus these various objections cannot also *simultaneously* apply to us, as they relate to different subject-matters.

Nor again can there be non-performance of those expiations which involve considerable hardships, through any fear of pain; because abandonment like that is to be avoided according to:

"Whatever act a man abandons, through fear of bodily pain, for the sole reason that it is painful,
Having made 'abandonment of passion', he does not get the fruit of abandonment." (*Gītā,* XVII.8)

Such texts as

"The very terrible sin of men in the Kali age which gives them the pain of hell,
At once gets dissolved when once He is remembered."
(*Viṣṇu Purāṇa,* VI.vii.10)

are directed to the remembrance of the Lord as their subject-matter.

Similarly, the reference to devotion as the subject-matter is made manifest by,

"Even if a man of very wicked life worships Me, worshipping none else,
He is certainly to be esteemed virtuous, for he has resolved aright.
Speedily he becomes of virtuous soul, he attains eternal peace;
Be assured, O son of Kuntī, My devotee never perishes."
(*Gītā,* IX.30, 31)

and so also by such texts as:

"The inhabitant of hell cried out 'O Kṛṣṇa.", "O Narasiṃha';
Thus was Viṣṇu celebrated by those in hell with devotion;
All the infernal tortures of those great-souled ones were destroyed."
(*Nṛsiṃha Purāṇa,* VIII.28, 29)

Here it is perceived that the celebration consisted in the mere pronunciation of the names; but not that by a word in the first case-ending, (celebrated) 'etc.' (e.g., remembrance, worship and the rest) is as a rule implied.—21

तत्स्थानत्वादनन्यधर्मः खले वालीवत् ।। २ । २ । २२ ।।

तत्स्थानत्वात् (*tat-sthāna-tvāt*), from standing in its place. अनन्यधर्मः (*an-anya-dharmaḥ*), not requiring the characteristics of the others. खले (*khale*), in a thrashing floor. वालीवत् (*vālī-vat*), like the post.

22. Because it stands in their place, it does not require their characteristics, just like the post in a thrashing floor.—77

In such declaration as "His best expiation is the one remembrance of Hari" (*Viṣṇu Purāṇa,* II.vi.34), the characteristics of the other expiations are, however, not to be understood by extending the application of the name 'expiation'; because it stands in the place of expiation, i.e., because it is enjoined in the place of expiation. Such is the meaning. Just as, in the injunction, "The post in a thrashing floor is the sacrificial post," (*Āśvalāyana Śrautasūtra,* IX.vii), there is the injunction for the use of the post in a thrashing floor as serving the purpose of the sacrificial post in tying up the animal, and there is no suggestion that the post in the thrashing floor to be so used should possess the characteristics of a sacrificial post, e.g., octagonal shape, etc.; so here the characteristics of an expiation such as the cutting of nails, hair, etc. do not make their appearance.

Nor is it to be said that the celebration of His names, etc., also are really expiations, as they are the causes of the destruction of sin. For it is to be considered that the word, expiation, is applicable in its primary sense to that which is of the form of penance, and that elsewhere it applies in a secondary sense,—according to the declaration:

"*Prāyaś* is said to be a name for penance, *citta* is said to be certainty;
It is recollected that *prāyaścitta* (expiation) is an act connected with
penance and certainty." (*Aṅgiras-smṛti*)—22

Now, as the subsidiaries are invariably present in the province of the principal, the province thereof is considered.

आनिन्द्ययोन्यधिक्रियते पारम्पर्यात् सामान्यवत् ।। २ । २ । २३ ।।

आनिन्द्ययोनि (*ā-nindya-yoni*), down to the lowest born. अधिक्रियते (*adhikriyate*), are included in, or are entitled to enter, the province of the higher devotion. पारम्पर्यात् (*pāramparyāt*), at second-hand, from one another. सामान्यवत् (*sāmānya-vat*), like universal knowledge.

23. (The province of the higher devotion) extends even to the lowest born, from one to another, like universal knowledge.—78

All including the blameworthy Cāṇḍāla and other castes are entitled to the practice of devotion, since there is no distinction in the universal desire to avoid the afflictions of worldly existence. Now, if you ask, how are those outside the three castes entitled to the practice of devotion, when they are not entitled to the study of the Veda?, to this the author replies "from one to another". According to the principle laid down in "*Dharma* or duty is the object the characteristic of which is instigation" (*Pūrvamīmāṃsā-sūtra,* I.i.2) and in "Because Brahman is to be known only through scriptures" (*Vedāntasūtra,* I.i.3), a transcendental object is to be known through the Śruti alone; this we do not dispute. But in the case of women, Śūdras, etc., by means of Itihāsa, Purāṇas, etc., and in the case of the Cāṇḍālas, etc., by the succession of instruction, in accordance with the Smṛti and usage of the excellent, knowledge also becomes really rooted in the Śruti; just as is their knowledge of such universal truths as the duty of not injuring any living being, etc.; as otherwise it would follow that this universal knowledge would not be found in them.—23

अतोह्यविपक्वभावानामपि तल्लोके ।। २ । २ । २४ ।।

अत: (*ataḥ*), hence. हि (*hi*), verily. अविपक्वभावानाम् (*a-vipakva-bhāvānam*), of those of unperfected devotin. अपि (*api*), even. तल्लोके (*tat-loke*) in His world.

24. Hence verily in His world (is the practice of devotion) even by those whose devotion has not been perfected.—79

Since it is the province of all, therefore verily is recollected the performance of the means of the higher devotion in the world of the Lord, i.e., in the Śvetadvīpa, by those whose higher devotion did not reach the state of perfection in this world. As for example, opening with the words:

"To the north of the ocean of milk lies the Śvetadvīpa of great splendour.
There intent on Nārayaṇa live men bright as the moon;
They are attached undividedly, and devoted to *Puruṣottama*."
(*Mahābharata,* Mokṣa Dharma, Nārāyaṇīya, CCCXXXVIII.12778-79)

their practice of the means of the higher devotion is revealed in such passages as:

"Then those men all together quickly ran up,
Folding their hands, full of joy, shouting salutation only;
Then I heard a great shout as they were discoursing together,
Lo: offering is presented to that God by those men."

(Ibid., CCCXXXVIII.12791-92)

It is clear therefore that the province of the higher devotion extends everywhere. Hence it has been aphorised. "The meditation on Brahman, according to the opinion of Bādarāyaṇa, must be admitted with regard to those also, who are above men, in the scale of evolution; because of its possibility with regard to them also (for they also have an organised body)." (*Vedāntasūtra,* I.iii.26)—24

Now, you may ask, why is not in His world the practice of the means of the higher devotion by those also whose devotion has attained a state of perfection? With this as an introduction, it is declared:

क्रमैकगत्युपपत्तेस्तु ।। २ । २ । २५ ।।

क्रमैकगत्युपपत्ते: (*krama-eka-gati-upapatteḥ*), from the proof of the successive and single stages or states. तु (*tu*), but.

25. But (there is not in His world the practice of the means of the higher devotion also by those whose devotion has attained the state of perfection), because there is proof of successive steps and of a single step.—80

And the word 'but' is for the purpose of pointing to the doubt which has arisen.

A description of successive steps is revealed in the same Nārāyaṇīya (the section relating to the worship of Nārāyaṇa): where, commencing with the words "Those who are exceedingly sinless in the word, devoid of virtue and vice" (*Mahābhārata,* Śānti Parva, CCXLVI.13383), and after describing the progress, by the door of the solar orb, successively into the bodies of Aniruddha, Pradyumna, and Saṃkarṣaṇa, it is declared:

"Whose minds are at rest in contemplation, who are self-restrained, whose senses are under control,
Who serve with undivided devotion, they enter Vāsudeva."

(Ibid., CCXLVI.13499)

Similarly, it is declared afterwards:

"But whose merits and demerits have been consumed as fuel, in the world, who are devoid of virtue and vice,
Their progress is, as defined by you, successively from one to another.

It is in the fourth stage that they attain the highest state.
Surely this religion of single-aimed devotion is the highest, and is dear to Nārāyaṇa,
Which enables men to attain the immutable Hari, without passing by the three (antecedent) stages." (Ibid., CCCL.13548-50)

This declaration of a single step is rightly established as having for its object of reference the devotion which has been perfected; as otherwise there would be contradiction between the two declarations. Therefore, the attainment of those respective worlds has reference to those whose devotion has not been perfected.—25

उत्क्रान्तिस्मृतिवाक्यशेषाच्च ।। २ । २ । २६ ।।

उत्क्रान्तिस्मृतिवाक्यशेषात् (*utkrānti-smṛti-vākya-śeṣāt*), from the conclusion of the declaration with departure and remembrance. च (*ca*), and.

26. (This distinction between perfect and imperfect devotion is proved) also from the conclusion of the declaration with 're-membrance' at the time of the *jīva*'s journey upwards.—81

In regard to the journey upwards, commencing with "endowed with devotion and the power of yoga," (*Gītā,* VIII.10), it is declared:

"Reciting the single-syllabled Brahman, *Aum*, remembering Me,
Who goes forth, abandoning the body, he attains the highest state." (*Gītā,* VIII.13)

And therein is the conclusion of the declaration.

The successive progress is thus declared:
"Fire, light, day, bright fortnight, six months of the sun's northern journey,
Going forth through those, men who know Brahman, reach Brahman." (*Gītā,* VIII.24)

Similarly, where the conclusion of the declaration is:

"All worlds up to the sphere of Brahmā, O Arjuna, are of a recurring nature;
But after coming near Me, O son of Kuntī, there is no re-birth." (Ibid., 16)

therefrom the introduction with the 'worlds' and also by the force of the word, *upa*, 'near', in "after coming near Me", the attainment of the worlds near to Him is rightly held to be only for those whose devotion has not been perfected. For him whose devotion has reached the state of perfection, even the going to His world as the fruit is not appropriate; because the fruit of such devotion is imperishable, and also because it is revealed that in His world there is the non-performance of the means. Moreover, if you were to say that from that world itself a gradual *mukti* would be secured to him whose devotion is imperfect, it would entail the futility of the injunction (in *Gītā,* VIII.13) about remembrance at the time of the *jīva*'s departure. Nor is thereby (i.e., by that injunction) the addition of the higher devotion implied; because there is positive knowledge that the higher devotion is the means of *mukti* independently of other means, namely:

"That supreme *Puruṣa,* O Pārtha, is to be attained by devotion independently of any other." (*Gītā,* VIII.22)

Therefore, even in His world there is the province of devotion. But in the land of the Bharatas (India) there is the only field for the production of meritorious works, according to the declaration:

"Certainly in no other field are works enjoined to mortals."
(*Viṣṇu Purāṇa,* II.iii.5)

But it has been declared before that devotion is not essentially a meritorious work (and is therefore independent of country). If you say that in other fields the subsidiaries of the higher devotion will not be available; we reply, no, because the principal itself being available, the subsidiaries are available, just like the subsidiary (fire) of the sacrifice of a Niṣāda king. Of the Śūdras, etc., on the other hand, the forbearance is from works arising out of Vedic *mantras,* but not from the means of devotion such as remembrance, celebration, etc. When by this much only their eligibility into the province of devotion is fulfilled, it is not right to suppose the application of learning as a preliminary condition.—26

Let then, you may say, even the great sinners be entitled to the higher devotion itself and also to the study of the Veda, etc., which are the subsidiaries of the means subsidiary to the higher devotion. To this the author replies.

महापातकिनां तवार्तौ ।। २ । २ । २७ ।।

महापातकिनां (*mahāpātakinām*), of the great sinners. तु (*tu*), but. आर्तौ (*ārtau*), in the devotion of the afflicted.

27. But of the great sinners (the province lies) in the devotion of affliction.—82

And of those who are addicted to sins which are the causes of fall, the province lies only in the devotion of affliction, as an expiation, and not elsewhere; because the destruction of those sins is of more importance than all else, according to the texts such as "Enjoying, one would increase sins". But on the removal of those sins their competence for the higher devotion is of course established.—27

Now the consideration of the single-aimed (perfect) devotion may give rise to the doubt whether all religion is different from the higher devotion. The author dispels this demon of a doubt.

सैकान्तभावो गीतार्थप्रत्यभिज्ञानात ।। २ । २ । २८ ।।

सा (*sā*), it, the higher devotion. एकान्तभावः (*eka-anta-bhāvaḥ*), single-aimed state or devotion. गीतार्थप्रत्यभिज्ञानात् (*Gītā-artha-pratyabhijñānāt*), from recognition as the meaning of the *Gītā.*

28. The higher devotion is the single-aimed devotion, as this is recognised to be the meaning of the *Gītā.*—83

'It', i.e., the higher devotion, it is that is called *ekāntabhāva* or the single-aimed devotion, and nothing else; why? because it is revealed that this is recognised as being the meaning of the *Gītā.* For example, in the Nārāyaṇīya itself there is the question:

"Those Brāhmaṇas who, thoroughly observant of religious practices, the Vedas with the Upaniṣads,
Read according to rules, and those also who are on the path of ascetics;
Superior to theirs I know the destination of the single-aimed men.
By whom has this religion been declared, by a god or by a seer?"
(*Mahābhārata,* Śānti Parva, Mokṣa Dharma, CCCL.13551, 52)

to which the answer is:

"When met in battle array the troops of the Kuru and Pāṇḍava hosts,
This was sung (*Gītā*) by the Lord himself to Arjuna depressed in mind."
(Ibid., 13554)

It is clear therefore that the state of having a single aim is the higher devotion.—28

Now, you may say, let the secondary forms of devotion also directly produce *mukti;* what harm is there in such an assumption? To this the author replies:

परां कृत्वैव सर्वेषां तथाह्याह ।। २ । २ । २६ ।।

परां (*parāṃ*), the higher. कृत्वा (*kṛtvā*), producing, एव (*eva*), only. सर्वेषां (*sarveṣāṃ*), of all. तथा (*tathā*), so. हि (*hi*), for. आह (*āha*), declares.

29. Only by producing the higher (devotion) (is the contribution) of all (towards *mukti*); for so He declares.—84

Only by producing the higher devotion is the contribution of all towards *mukti.* For so the Lord declares, adding at the same time the reason:

"Whoever shall declare this exceeding mystery to those who are devoted to Me,
Having produced the higher devotion to Me, he will without doubt attain to Me alone." (*Gītā,* XVIII.68)

Here if you were to hold the meaning to be nothing but this that the fruit of instructing that religion is also the attainment of the state of Brahman, then what would be the object of the declaration "having produced the higher devotion to Me?" seeing that the higher devotion is revealed by the Śruti as being the means of *mukti.* For the same reason, in the case of Uparicara Vasu, by the words "His own kingdom, wealth, etc." (vide aphorism 44, commentary) has been exhibited the mark of devotion in the form of affection for the Supreme Lord; because such regard cannot have a purpose of its own (but must serve the purpose of something higher than itself). Therefore the intention is inferred that the contribution which all those means that have been revealed as being the causes of *mukti,* make towards *mukti* is by the production of the higher devotion. Nor could these means produce both (i.e., the higher devotion and also *mukti*); because being acts, they cannot produce *mukti.* And so also the declaration comes to have reference to an object which is visible (i.e., the higher devotion and not to an object which invisible, i.e., *mukti*).—29

Here ends the second lecture of the second chapter in the commentary on the One Hundred Aphorisms of Śāṇḍilya composed by the most learned teacher Svapneśvara.

CHAPTER III

The Object of Worship

LECTURE I: The Nature of Brahman

Since the excellence of devotion depends on the excellence of the object of worship, and since the devotee attains to His state, the object of worship is here described.

भजनीयेनाद्वितीयमिदं कृत्स्नस्य तत्स्वरूपत्वात ।। ३ । १ । १ ।।

भजनीयेन (*bhajanīyena*), by the object of worship. अद्वितीयम् (*a-dvitīyam*), un-seconded. इदं (*idaṃ*), it, the creation, the object of knowledge. कृत्स्नस्य (*kṛtsna-sya*), of the whole. तत्स्वरूपत्वात् (*tat-svarūpa-tvāt*), from being that the essential form of which is that, i.e., the object of worship.

1. The object of knowledge is not seconded by the object of worship, because it has this as its essential form.—85

The proof or existence of the object to be known is dependent on knowledge; this is the conclusion of all systems (*tantra*) of self-culture. Knowledge is existence. Existence is not a *jāti* or genus (as the Nyāya-Vaiśeṣikas hold) because there can be no genus in a genus, etc., (whereas existence pervades all generic as well as specific principles). Even if genus could exist in genus, there can be no supposition of the desired relation (of *samavāya* or 'combination'), in view of the fault of redundancy. Therefore, knowledge is the Supreme Brahman which by itself pervades everywhere. In every visible object there is non-difference from it; while the difference of the visible objects is insofar as they are other than existent. If you say that there would then be such intuitions as "A jar is knowledge," just as there is the intuition "A jar is existent," we reply that this will depend on whether the idea of its essential form is or is not present, since a jar does not present itself to the senses as being real (but as having a transitory existence only). If you say that Brahman possesses knowledge, desire, and effort of will and that these are the causes of the material cause of creation; we reply that there is great simplicity in the supposition that they are causes along with and insofar as they co-exist with the material cause. And this Brahman, co-existing with the material cause (i.e., *māyā*), is verily not a substratum of qualities,* as such a supposition is redundant. The supposition of its being the knower, etc., is caused by the *upādhis* or external circumstances, as in the case of time (the division of which into moments, hours, days, nights, etc., is due to external circumstances).—1

तच्छक्तिर्माया जडसामान्यात् ।। ३ । १ । २ ।।

तच्छक्तिः (*tat-śaktiḥ*), its power. माया (*māyā*), *māyā,* ignorance, limitation. जडसामान्यात् (*jaḍa-sāmānyāt*), from its being the summum genus of all insensate things.

2. Its power is *māyā*, from its being the summum genus, of all insensate things.—86

'Its' i.e., of Brahman, the power of lordliness is sung as *māyā*:

"Verily this My *māyā* divine, constituted by the three *guṇas*, is difficult to pass beyond.
Who take refuge in Me alone, they cross over this Māyā."
(*Gītā,* VII.14)

"With Me as the superintendent *Prakṛti* brings forth things movable and immovable.
Through My superintendence, O son of Kuntī, the world appears and disappears." (Ibid., IX.10)

Its power is called *māyā,* from the variety of its effects, and not from their unreality; since the Śruti revealing the existence of Brahman is for the purpose of establishing the existence of the effect, i.e., the world. It is not proper to hold that they are unreal, also because their unreality would entail the unreality of their cause (i.e., *māyā*). If you say that the being unreal consists in being liable to be opposed by the knowledge of the principles (so that only the principles are real, and their products are unreal); we reply, no, their unreality itself being unreal, (as some of you Vedāntins hold), their reality is only more firmly established;** on the other hand, if you say that their (apparent) unreality is real, then the reality of visible objects is obtained. And (further) since there can be no manifestation of what is unreal, reality must always belong to objects which are to be manifested (by Brahman). What is called the manifestation of a snake, etc., in a piece

*"He is not the possessor of knowledge, a desire to create, and will as the Nyāya would maintain; he is himself pure knowledge."—Cowell

**"One of the cardinal tenets of the Vedānta is that the ignorance which cause the world, is itself false as being imagined by ignorance; but if so, the falsity of a falsity is *truth* as *minus* into *minus* gives *plus.*"—Cowell of rope, that is nothing but a mistake (lit. the manifestation of one thing as another), since this mistake is contradicted or is not contradicted by the existence or non-existence of the other thing.

That *māyā* is the summum genus of all insensate things; this genus is capable of being known and is really eternal; otherwise there would be no regularity or uniformity (i.e., the thing to be known would be both existent and non-existent). Hence follows the eternality of the intelligent and the non-intelligent.—2

व्यापकत्वाद्व्याप्यानाम् ।। ३ । १ । ३ ।।

व्यापकत्वात् (*vyāpaka-tvāt*), from the pervadingness, व्याप्यानाम् (*vyāpyānām*), of the pervaded.

3. From the pervadingness of the pervaded (proceeds creation).—87

Similarly, from the pervading or general principles is the production of the pervaded or special principles; for the general principles are regarded as being the material causes of the special principles through identity with them, and by no means by the relation called *samavāya* or intimate relation or combination, as in that case there would be redundancy in the consequent supposition first of a difference and next of a relation between two different things; i.e. the cause and the effect. So too (on our theory of identity) is the convention or explanation of words simpler on the maxim of 'taking by the horn' (i.e., the maxim that in controlling an unruly ox or the like you should first somehow manage to take it by one horn, and then bring it under complete control by seizing it by the other horn in such texts as '*uktha* is Brahman', etc.). By existence in all effects is the (material and not the efficient) causality of the Supreme Lord; for the efficient or instrumental causality belongs to His Intelligence from its penetrating all objects which are to be known. But since it belongs to intelligence (*buddhi*) which is to be illumined by the Witness (the soul) not to be known by a function of itself, the instrumental casuality will be possible in the case of intelligence which is capable of being known by itself, although the character of the principle properly called intelligence (i.e., the character of not being known by itself) is absent from it.

Having slept when the Lord awakes after a cosmic dissolution, at first there is the production of intelligence; having contemplated (by intelligence) the relations of cause and effect, etc., He, the Lord, creates. Although intelligence has (then) no object of its own, still from being the proximate condition of consciousness, like the oil, etc., in the lamp, it possesses manifestation in a particular manner. Then takes place the production of *ahaṃkāra* or egoism from the resolution "I will make", as appears from declarations in the Śruti and Smṛti such as "He resolved, 'I shall be many' " (*Chāndogya Upaniṣad*, VI.2). Since *ahaṃkāra* penetrates the transformations of *buddhi* such as desire, etc., it too is a single (original) principle. But in this as a principle resides *buddhi*, since *buddhi* is of a more general character. 'I am the lord, being produced by an effort of will',—such is *ahaṃkāra*; because it is produced by an effort of will and because it is constantly determined by this. *Ahaṃkāra* also is (in turn) therefore the cause of the subtle elements, the gross elements, the senses, etc. Among these again it is the general principles called the 'forms' of sound, touch, form, taste, and smell that are in turn the causes of the gross elements in which sound, etc., reside. If you say that in that case there should be the apprehension of all the principles everywhere; we reply that their apprehension takes place in the same way as does the apprehension of the genus in the apprehension of the individual transformations belonging to the genus. Such is the successive interpeneration of the general principles in the special ones; and it is thus clear that all the principles beginning with Brahman are the material causes of a jar, for example. Nor is it proper to say that although the principles are the immediate antecedents of the effect, i.e., creation, since there can be no creation without action, therefore action is the cause and not the principles; because material causality depends on the identity of the cause and effect; but if the principles were not the causes then creation would follow the rule of non-identity of cause and effect. Moreover, since the causal principles are thus the means of *mukti*, there is the creation of the intelligence, etc., of the living beings, not identically with one another, but separately for each individual. Since there is no *buddhi* anywhere which can take or has taken cognizance of a cosmic dissolution, etc., from the start of creation in the beginning of a cosmic cycle, during deep sleep there is a dissolution of the *jīvas*, intelligences; in *mukti* this dissolution is without end.—3

Now, it is not right to hold with the non-deistic Sāṃkhyas that creation proceeds from the principle, intelligence because of succession and because of absence of proof. To this effect is declared the aphorism.

न प्राणिबुद्धिभ्योऽसम्भवात् ।। ३ । १ । ४ ।।

न (*na*), not. प्राणिबुद्धिभ्यः (*prāṇi-buddhi-bhyaḥ*), from the intelligences of living beings. असम्भवात् (*a-sambhavāt*), from impossibility.

4. (Creation proceeds) not from the intelligences of the living beings because this is impossible.—88

The successive creation of gods, seers, etc., has been revealed in the Śruti. From whose intelligence will be produced this creation of the gross elements? It follows therefore that there is the Lord endowed with intelligence.—4

निर्मायोच्चावचं श्रुतीश्च निर्मिमीते पितृवत् ।। ३ । १ । ५ ।।

निर्माय (*nirmāya*), having created. उच्चावचं (*uccā-avacam*), high and low. श्रुतीः (*śrutīḥ*), Śrutis, the Vedas. च (*ca*) also. निर्मिमीते (*nirmimīte*), creates. पितृवत् (*pitṛ-vat*), like a father.

5. Having created high and low, He also creates the Vedas, like a father.—89

Having created beings high and low according to their merits and demerits, He creates the Vedas through His desire for their good. Just as a father, having begotten sons, also by teachings makes known to them what was not known to them, viz., the attainment of good and the avoidance of evil, so also does He, the Lord.—5

मिश्रोपदेशान्नेति चेन्न स्वल्पत्वात् ।। ३ । १ । ६ ।।

मिश्रोपदेशात् (*miśra-upadeśāt*), from mixed instruction. न (*na*), not. इति (*iti*), thus. चेत् (*cet*), if. न (*na*), no. स्वल्पत्वात् (*su-alpa-tvāt*), from the extreme smallness.

6. (If you say that) since the instructions are of a mixed character, (He is) not (like a father), we reply, no, because the fruit of the mixed instruction is altogether insignificant.—90

Now, if you say that this Lord is not really benevolent like a father, because His instructions about sacrifices are mixed with acts of injury to living beings which are the means of producing sin; we reply, no, for, since in comparison with the happiness, etc., which are the fruit of the principal portion of the sacrifice, the fruit of the injury involved in the subsidiary is insignificant, the enjoiner of this is not on this account other than benevolent. But, you may say, since injury as the subsidiary of the sacrifice has the same fruit as that of the principal (i.e., the sacrifice), it does not fall within the scope of the general prohibition against injury; otherwise the two injunctions, viz., to do injury in special sacrifices and to abstain from doing injury generally, would be in the nature of alternatives and thereby give to the performer the option of doing or of not doing; therefore, the general prohibition should be held to apply where there is no special injunction, as in the case of *āhavanīya* (where the general rule is suspended by the special rule which is only an ancillary part of the *upanayana*, see *Jaiminīya Nyāyamālāvistāra*, VI.viii.2). To this we reply that the non-opposition between the two injunctions consists in this only that injury as a subsidiary is the cause of *apūrva* (or evil desert which ripens into activity afterwards) and that injury in general is the cause of sin.

Now, if the special injury in a sacrifice is the cause of some desired fruit unmixed with the evil of predominant pain, this sense of the special injunction, when connected with the negative prefix (as in the general prohibition) will you may say, be expressive of the absence thereof (i.e., of injury in special cases being the cause of some desired fruit, etc.); so that the injunction "Let one not do injury to all living beings", will be the primary cause of pain. To this we reply that it is true that the pain which arises from the injury which is the subsidiary of a sacrifice, is not predominant; that since it is invariably accompanied by the happiness, etc., which are the fruits of the principal sacrifice, it is not an obstacle to the performance of the act of injury; otherwise, there would be an illicit extension of the rule, owing to the indeterminateness, of the idea of predominance. Therefore 'predominance' in the case of pains is a particular genus or general characteristic which admits of differentiations (in individual causes). In the case of death by suicide as an act of expiation, etc., or in the case of death by suicide at Prayāga (at the confluence of the three rivers in Allahabad), the pain caused by the act of suicide is light in comparison to the fruits of such deaths. Hence verily *Pañcaśikhā* also enjoins *pratiavamarśa*, i.e., that this pain is to be borne with patience; this injunction is because the pain is altogether, insignificant, and not because it is predominant. Where the pain is predominant, there the Śrutis themselves have shown the exculpatory rites of carrying a firebrand from the *āhavanīya* fire three times round the victim. In the Smṛtis also it has been declared that "there are places for the householders" (*Manusaṃhitā*, III.68). This is not the declaration of an exception to a general injunction nor does it apply to one who has no household; therefore, to quote from the *Viṣṇu Purāṇa*, III.vi.21, "Whom shall the man who lives by playing and killing fly for refuge?"—6

Now, from the mention of the Śruti, the *apūrva* resulting from the rites enjoined in the Śrutis, is being considered: Does it belong to the performer, does it belong to the enjoyer, or does it belong to the Supreme Lord?

फलमस्माद्बादरायणो दृष्टत्वात् । ३ । १ । ७ ।।

फलम् (*phalam*), fruit. अस्मात् (*asmāt*), from Him. बादरायण: (*bādarāyaṇaḥ*, Bādarāyaṇa, Vyāsa. दृष्टत्वात् (*dṛṣṭa-tvāt*), from being seen.

7. The fruit comes from Him, says Bādarāyaṇa, because it is seen (to be so in common life).—91

As it is seen that the fruits of actions come from the pleasure and displeasure of the king, etc., for whom the actions are performed, so it is from this Brahman that, says the lord Bādarāyaṇa, the fruit of prescribed works comes (see the *Vedāntasūtra*. I.i.2).

The fruit does not accrue to the performer, because it is seen that the fruit of the ceremonies performed by a father after the birth of a son, accrues to the son. Now, if you say that the enjoyment of the fruit accrues to the enjoyer, it is to be considered who the enjoyer exactly is to whom the enjoyment accrues; for if the two terms (i.e., enjoyer and enjoyment) were thus wholly dependent on each other for their significance, there would arise the fault of 'mutual dependence' or arguing in a circle. Therefore, since it is seen to be so in common life, the attainment of the fruit, good or evil, is from the pleasure and displeasure of the Supreme Lord, and it will accrue to the subject for whom the fruit is intended by Him. Nor again need the accrual of the attainment of the fruit to the subject for whom it is intended entail the supposition of a fresh act producing an additional *apūrva*; if it were not so, an *apūrva* would be entailed also in the case of the service, etc., rendered to the king. Hence it is that works are revealed in the Śruti only as giving pleasure to the Lord (and not as producing an *apūrva*). Thus:

"But who follow out this ambrosial religion in the manner declared,
Full of faith, intent on Me, those devotees are exceedingly dear to Me."
(*Gītā,* XII.20)

In spite of the existence of pleasure and displeasure in Him, it does not belong to the Lord to be a *saṃsārī,* i.e., one who undergoes the revolutions of births and deaths and experiences of the fruits of works; for He is all that exists, He is above all pain, and He is eternally free.—7

व्युत्क्रमादप्ययस्तथा दृष्टम् ।। ३ । १ । ८ ।।

व्यत्क्रमात् (*vyutkramāt*), from regression, in the reverse order. अप्यय: (*api-ayaḥ*), going away, dissolution. तथा (*tathā*), similarly, so. दृष्टम् (*dṛṣṭam*), seen.

8. Dissolution is through resilience, for so is it seen (to be in ordinary life).—92

Dissolution is held to be through the resilience of the special principles into the general ones; because it is seen that the dissolution of a jar and like special forms is through their resolution into the general form of earth.—8

Here ends the first lecture of the third chapter in the commentary on the One Hundred Aphorism of Śāṇḍilya composed by the most learned teacher Svapneśvara.

LECTURE II: The Relation of the Jīva and Brahman

Mukti is described as the *jīvas* attaining Brahma-hood. The determination of the object of worship is continued in this lecture also by discriminating the nature thereof (i.e., of the *jīva* and Brahman). By raising the doubt how the one happens to be the other, the author of the aphorisms declares the fitness of the *jīvas* for the state of the Lord.

तदैक्यं नानात्वैकत्वमुपाधियोगहानादादित्यवत् ।। ३ । २ । १ ।।

तदैक्यं (*tat-aikyaṃ*), its unity. नानात्वैकत्वम् (*nānā-tva-ekatvaṃ*), manifoldness or oneness. उपाधियोगहानात् (*upādhi-yoga-hānāt*), through conjunction or disjunction of the proximate condition or adjunct. आदित्यवत् (*āditya-vat*), like the sun.

1. Its unity (appears as) manifoldness or oneness according to the conjunction or disjunction of the adjunct; as is the case with the sun.—93

According to:

"All this verily is Brahman, nothing manifold is here."

Chāndogya Upaniṣad, III.14

"Just as the single sun illumines the whole of this world,
So does, O Bhārata, the owner of the field (soul) illumine the whole of the field (body)." (*Gītā,* XIII.34)

"Know Me also, O Bhārata, to be the knower of the field in all the fields." (Ibid., XIII.33)

it is unity that is the nature of Brahman or the Self. The intuition of the Self again is bothways, i.e., both as unity and as multiplicity. This intuition caused by the intelligence which is the adjunct of the *jīva* is reflected in the soul. And so declares the Śruti:

"It is seen as one and also as many, like the moon in water.

As the one sky is seen under the diversities of white, blue, etc.
So by those whose vision is misguided is the self also, though it is one, seen to be as different individuals." (*Viṣṇu Purāṇa*, II.xvi.22)

Then when the intelligence which is the adjunct of the *jīva* is destroyed by the higher devotion, the oneness comes out again, and in this there is no contradiction. Just as does the oneness of the sun which is of the nature of light come out on the removal of the mirror, etc., which are the external causes of its reflections, so is it here.—1

पृथगिति चेन्न परेणासम्बन्धात् प्रकाशानाम्।।३।२।२।।

पृथक् (*pṛthak*), separate, distinct. इति (*iti*), thus. चेत् (*cet*), if. न (*na*), no. परेण (*pareṇa*), with the other. असम्बन्धात् (*a-sambandhāt*), from want of connection. प्रकाशानाम् (*prakāśānām*), of the lights, of the souls as self-manifesting.

2. If (you say that the souls should be) distinct, (we reply), no, because (then the souls as) self-manifesting (would have) no connection with the other.—94

If you say that the *jīvas* must be 'distinct' i.e., absolutely different from one another, and must by their very nature manifest themselves, because otherwise there could be no such rule that such a soul was released and such a soul was bound, we reply, no, for although it might be possible for the non-deistic Sāṃkhyas to somehow maintain this view, it is impossible for the deistic Sāṃkhyas to do so. How so? Because, by their being of the nature of light, as supposed by you, they would reveal themselves by their own light, and would thus lack the connection with the 'other', i.e., the Supreme Lord, defined as that of the seer and the object to be seen, as they would not require to be illumined by Him, just as lamps, etc., are not illumined by the sun. So that it would accrue to Brahman not to be the Lord, not to be all-knowing, and to be an object to be known (by the self-manifesting souls). Nor are the souls such as are to be illumined from the outside, as in that case it would follow that they themselves are non-intelligent (according to the maxim that whatever is illumined by another that is non-intelligent). Nor are they to be illumined by the mutual functions of their intelligences, for their illumination takes place only by the subjugation of *tamas* and not really by the function of the *sattva* present in the internal organ. Nor is illumination possible in the case of a thing which is not suited to illumination, for certainly one lamp is not capable of being illumined by another lamp, even on the removal of the veil (e.g., curtain) between them. Thus there is a certain common, though non-essential, attribute between the external and internal lights (i.e., the lamp and soul), whereby it appears that the word 'light' is used in a secondary sense in such texts as "Verily this soul (*Puruṣa*) is its own light" (*Bṛhadāraṇyaka Upaniṣad*, IV.iii.9). Therefore, it is under the characteristic of being the illuminator of the world that the self which is pure consciousness is proved to exist or established; hence there is in this no dependence on anything else. Moreover, incontestable indeed is the proof of the existence of the soul also by the fact of its being the receptacle (of the reflections) of the attributes of mind, viz., error and knowledge of the principles; while it is in a secondary sense that the functions of the intelligence are spoken of as being knowledge and pleasure.

"What proof is there that souls are distinct? Only the difference of the principles of intelligence exists
To account for the different situations of bondage and release.
Where are these in the case of the souls that are eternally free?"—2

Now, refuting the view that souls which are existences are certainly subject to modifications, and that knowledge, desire, etc., are their attributes, because there are such intuitions as 'I know', 'I desire', 'I am happy', etc., the author declares:

न विकारिणस्तु करणविकारात् ।। ३ । २ । ३ ।।

न (*na*), not. विकारिण: (*vikāriṇaḥ*), subject to modification. तु (*tu*), but. करणविकारात् (*karaṇa-vikārāt*), from the modification of the instrument.

3. But (the souls are) not subject to modification, because the modification is of the instrument (i.e., the internal organ).—95

The souls do not deserve to be possessed of the modifications of knowledge, etc. Why? Because, since knowledge, etc., are explained as belonging to that which is the instrument of the perception of pleasure, etc., it follows that the souls are not liable to modification. For, thus, in such inferences as "the perception of pleasure must be through an instrument", since the connection of such an instrument exists by the relation of identity (with the effect), pleasure, etc., are not the modifications of the soul. This is established also from the inference that like fairness, etc., pleasure and the like do not belong to the soul but are perceived as reflected in the soul. Similarly, it is by means of identity with its cause (*ahaṃkāra*) that the mind assumes the character of egoism; there is no such assumption of egoism by the mind when it is dissolved during deep sleep. This is just like the attributes of the nature of time to the *upādhis* or external circumstances which cause the divisions of time. This is enough.—3

Now, in regard to the possible enquiry, how Brahma-hood accrues to the *jīva*, the author declares—

अनन्यभक्त्या तद्बुद्धिर्बुद्धिलयादत्यन्तम् ।। ३ । २ । ४ ।।

अनन्यभक्त्या (*an-anya-bhaktyā*), by single-aimed devotion. तद्बुद्धिः (*tat-buddhiḥ*), the knowledge thereof, i.e., of the identity of the *jīva* with Brahman. बुद्धिलयात् (*buddhi-layāt*), through the dissolution of intelligence. अत्यन्तम् (*atyantam*), absolute, final.

4. Through the final dissolution of intelligence by means of single-aimed devotion, there arises the knowledge of the identity of the *jīva* with Brahman.—96

It has been revealed:

"By single-aimed devotion is to be attained, O Pārtha, that Supreme *Puruṣa*,
In whom all created things reside, by whom all this is pervaded."
(*Gītā*, VIII.22)

Similarly (in the *Nṛsiṃha Purāṇa*, it is recollected):

"When the ancient *Puruṣa* is to be attained by devotion alone, wherefore is not an effort made for *mukti*?"

Therefore the meaning is that *mukti* characterised as the attainment of the bliss of Brahman results when the final dissolution of intelligence takes place by the higher devotion as soon as it arises in the *jīva*. By intelligence here is meant the adjunct of the *jīva*, since it has been declared that the principle, Intelligence, belongs to the Lord alone. And thus is indicated the definition of *mukti* in this form that *mukti* is the attainment of the bliss of Brahman co-existing with the antecedent non-existence of the dissolution of his intelligence.

If you say that since the attainment of the bliss of Brahman is a thing accomplished (as all souls are identical in nature with Brahman), it cannot be an object of volition; we reply, no, because it is an object of voluntary pursuit when accompanied with the knowledge that it is such, as in the case of the village, etc., (the mere existence of which does not prevent their being objects of acquisition for which one makes effort not because they exist but only when they are known to be objects worth acquiring).

Otherwise, since such, namely, "This is pleasure, herein is the being pleasure (i.e., the genus of pleasure," is knowledge, and since genus is eternal, the thing (i.e., pleasure) which possessed that genus would also come to be not an object of volition, because desire and effort of will do not possess the distinctions of knowledge that this is pleasure and that herein is the being pleasure. Therefore it follows that desire and effort of will take place in respect of even an object which is already in existence, under colour of that aspect of it which is not yet in existence. If you say that the knowledge that it is not to be accomplished by an effort of will is an obstacle to the exercise of desire and effort of will; we ask, is it contrary to reason to suppose that desire and effort of will come into play by overshadowing by a violent passion even the fact that the desired end is not to be accomplished by an effort of will, just as in the case of the hawk-sacrifice the performance of which is possible through the overshadowing of the knowledge that it will be accompanied by a predominant evil consequence, (by the violent anger towards an enemy; cf. "Let him who desires to kill his enemy by incantation offer the hawk-sacrifice."—*Ṣaḍviṃśa Brāhmaṇa*, III.8)?

Also from the *Āgama*:

"Bliss is the form of Brahman and that is founded in *mukti*."

it is known for certain that the attainment of the bliss of Brahman is an object of voluntary pursuit.—4

You may say that just as, notwithstanding the production of the higher devotion, there is still the experience of the *adṛṣṭa* or merit and demerit which determine the duration of life, till it exhausts itself, so it is by experience alone that there can be the dissolution of the other *apūrvas* or merits and demerits; and that therefore there can be nothing but the absence of *mukti*. To this the author replies:

आयुश्चिरमितरेषां तु हानिरनास्पदत्वात् ।। ३ । २ । ५ ।।

आयु: (*āyuḥ*), life. चिरम् (*ciram*), lasting. इतरेषां (*itareṣāṃ*), of the rest. तु (*tu*), but. हानि: (*hāniḥ*), destruction, abolition, अनास्पदत्वात् (*an-āspada-tvāt*), through being seatless.

5. Life lasts, but of the rest there is abolition through their becoming site-less.—97

When affection for the Self is produced,

"Only so long is his duration as he shall not be delivered; then he shall be accomplished." (*Chāndogya Upaniṣad*, VI.xiv.2)

"What has he to do with merit, wealth and desire? *Mukti* is present in the palm of his hand,
Whose devotion is firm in Thee, the root of all worlds."
(*Viṣṇu Purāṇa,* I.xx.27)

And thus 'life,' i.e., the *adṛṣṭa* which determines the duration of life, just only so long as it lasts, becomes an obstacle to *mukti*, even when the higher devotion has been produced; just only so long is the state called *jīvan-mukti* or *mukti* in lifetime. As regards the other merits and demerits, since on the dissolution of the *adṛṣṭa* determining the duration of life there is the final dissolution of the individual intelligence (where the higher devotion has been produced) and consequently there is the absence of the site of experience, it is the absence of their experience in the individual intelligence that results; hence it does not follow that there can be nothing but the absence of *mukti*, because the intelligence also, by virtue of its being so modified, is a cause of *mukti* (in a negative way). Nor do those merits and demerits thereby cease to be causes; because the causality of a thing is not impaired even where there is the non-production of the fruit in the absence of other (concurrent) causes. (If you say that some *adṛṣṭa* will be still left in the form of the pleasure and displeasure of the Lord, see aphorism 91, we reply, no, because) dissolution also of the *adṛṣṭa* in the form of the pleasure and displeasure of the Lord will take place either in the course of time or from the general cause of a cosmic dissolution (when it occurs), just as there is the dissolution of the *adṛṣṭas* produced by the subsidiaries of a sacrifice when through some flaw in any of the subsidiaries they fail to produce the ultimate *adṛṣṭa* which was the aim of the sacrifice as a whole and to which they were contributing. The surrender to the Lord, on the other hand, of works which are the obstacles to *mukti*, is for the sake of absence or cancellation of bondage by them. Thus all is clear. It is in a mediate way (i.e., through devotion) that destruction of the effects of works takes place by means of the fire of knowledge.—5

Now, you may ask, is the *saṃsāra* of the *jīva* held to be caused by absence of knowledge or to be caused by absence of devotion? In regard to this proceeds this aphorism:

संसृतिरेषामभक्तिः स्यान्नाज्ञानात् कारणासिद्धेः ।। ३ । २ । ६ ।।

संसृतिः (*saṃsṛtiḥ*), *saṃsāra*, transmigration, worldly existence. एषाम्

(*eṣām*), of these. अभक्तिः (*a-bhaktiḥ*), absence of devotion. स्यात् (*syāt*), must be. न (*na*), not. अज्ञानात् (*a-jñānāt*), from absence of knowledge. कारणासिद्धेः (*kāraṇa-a-siddheḥ*), from non-existence or non-proof as cause.

6. Their *saṃsāra* is (from) absence of devotion, and not from absence of knowledge, because there is no proof of it as a cause.—98

Heaven, *mukti* in lifetime, and *mukti*, such is their threefold state. *Mukti* in lifetime is the higher devotion; while its non-existence is *saṃsāra*. It is only from the absence of the desires of devotion that *saṃsāra* persists; it ceases, when devotion is produced; and so it has been declared by the great seers:

"So long are there affliction, and that desire, so long delusion as well as sorrow,
So long does not a man take refuge in Thee, the abolisher of infinite sin."
(*Viṣṇu Purāṇa*, I.ix.72-73)

Creation is caused by the absence of the knowledge of the principles; by knowledge is its abolition desired; because in the absence (through knowledge) of the causes of the mistake of a rope for a snake the mistake is impossible. Births, the scourgings of the dreadful attendants of Yama, those sufferings, the sights of the son of the Sun, these are the consequences of the creature turning away from the lotus of Kṛṣṇa's feet, being led astray by the mirage of the wave of the 'I' and 'Mine' of *ahaṃkāra*.—6

त्रीण्येषां नेत्राणि शब्दलिङ्गाक्षभेदाद्रुद्रवत् ।। ३ । २ । ७ ।।

त्रीणि (*trīṇi*), three. एषां (*eṣām*) their. नेत्राणि (*netrāṇi*), eyes. शब्दलिङ्गाक्षभेदात् (*śabda-liṅga-akṣa-bhedāt*), according to the differences of 'word' or authoritative declaration, mark of inference, and the senses. रुद्रवत् (*rudra-vat*), like Rudra.

7. Like Rudra, they have three eyes, distinguished as authoritative declaration, mark of inference, and the senses.—99

'Their', i.e., of the *jīvas,* there are three eyes as instruments, that is to say, serving as proofs in respect of certain knowledge of objects. Although there is no distinction in the certain knowledge which they severally produce, it is considered as being threefold according to the threefoldness of the instruments. These instruments are as follows: The instrument of certain knowledge which is caused by authoritative declaration is the word in the form of an object denoted by a word to which the word is appropriate and which is understood. It is mentioned first (in the aphorism) in order to declare its superiority (to the other two) consisting in its being the means, etc., of transcendental devotion. So again the instrument of certain knowledge which is caused by inference is the knowledge of the mark of inference abiding in the subject of the inference (i.e., the minor term) and accompanied or pervaded by a known major term. Since according to us an effect pre-exists in the cause, the fact of its being known in the process of inference is also not incompatible. The instruments of certain knowledge which is caused by sense-perception (internal and external) are the sense-organs when they are in contact with objects; and they, i.e., the mind, and the organs of hearing, touch, sight, taste and smell, six in number, having overcome the *tamas* of the internal organ by their respective contacts, produce the function of the *sattva* (of the internal organ) which assumes the form of the object as illumined by the Conscious Self. Hence it is declared:

"Illumination arises in all the gateways of this body."

(*Gītā*, XIV.11)

But the modifications such as pain, etc., of the mind which has the form of the *jīva*'s intelligence, do not remain uncognised; it is by the light of the Self therefore that they are illumined. Hence, to avoid redundancy, we do not make the supposition of a function of the *sattva* in their case. Only in this sense are they said to be illumined by the Witness.

Thus then there are only three proofs distinguished as word, inference and sense-perception; just as Rudra has three seats of sight, neither more nor less, so is it here and their signs are (in both the cases) the characteristics of their being of the forms of the moon, sun, and fire.*

Comparison, again, is not a separate proof, but is included in the three proofs themselves, because it is for the purpose only of comprehending the force or direct meaning of a word, and this is possible, with the help of the mind also together with the inference called *sāmānyato dṛṣṭa* or commonly seen, since in this case the word the force of which is to be ascertained is coextensive with some well-known word, as in the case of the definition

*"Śiva's right eye is the sun, his left is the moon, and his third eye in the centre of his forehead is fire. I suppose that the sun properly stands for revelation as being the brightest, the moon for inference (from its connection with *pakṣa* as the 'lunar fortnight' and 'the minor term') and the five fires for the five senses. In the text, however, the moon is put first in the compound (according to the rule *abhyarhitam ca*) as being the monarch of the stars, planets and Brahmans." See Cowell, *Viṣṇu Purāṇa*, I.xxii.

of the poet and poem.

The investigation of proofs has been discussed by us in our *Nyāya-tattvanikaṣa* and *Vedāntatattvanikaṣa;* so it is not elaborated here.

The intelligence of the *jīva* is named the mind; it undergoes contraction and expansion; whereby the simultaneity and non-simultaneity of cognitions are explained.

Since from the play of the *ahaṃkāra* of the Lord is the production of the intelligences of the *jīvas,* in intelligence egoism also, like pain, etc., is directly perceived.

Since the production of the subtile elements, the gross elements, the senses, etc., is from the intelligence of the Lord, and since they are to be known by the intelligence of the Lord, this is capable of being apprehended by Consciousness as well as by the senses.

The five gross elements, the five subtile elements, the eleven senses (of cognition and action), *ahaṃkāra,* intelligence, the *Pradhāna,* the soul, and the Supreme Lord, such is the collection of the principles. These are the twenty-six principles.—7

आविस्तिरोभावाः विकाराः स्युः क्रियाफलसंयोगात् ।। ३ । २ । ८ ।।

आविस्तिरोभावाः (*āvis-tiras-bhāvāḥ*), appearances and disappearances. विकाराः (*vikārāḥ*), modifications. स्युः (*syuḥ*), are, should be. क्रियाफलसंयोगात् (*kriyā-phalasaṃyogāt*), from the conjunction of action and fruit.

8. Creation and destruction are changes of form of that which exists, because there is conjunction of action with object.—100

As a collateral subject, creation and dissolution are considered. Of these creation characterised as appearance or evolution is of the existent alone, and consists in its capability of undergoing change; similarly, dissolution characterised as disappearance or involution is also of the existent alone, and consists in its incapability of undergoing change. Likewise increase, decrease, etc., are nothing but changes of form of that which exists. How so? Because there is predication of the connection with the fruit (i.e., the effect or the object) of the meaning of the verb in such instances as "He makes a jar," "He destroys a jar," etc., and these connections can occur only in the case of that which exists, and not in the case of that which does not exist. And so has it been declared:

> "There is no production of that which exists not, there is no destruction of that which exists." (*Gītā,* II.16)

Likewise, in such instances also as "It is produced," "It is destroyed," etc. the object is perceived to be the seat of the change expressed by the verbs, and this, i.e., to be the seat of the changes, is possible only in the case of that which exists.

Appearance or evolution, again, means connection with the initial moment, the meaning of which is that it is the counter-opposite of destruction, because there is no determinate sense in which the word initial can be applied to a moment (since the process of creation is infinite both towards the beginning and towards the end). Nor can you say that as it is necessary that every appearance must have another (antecedent) appearance, the faults of infinite regression and redundancy, one or other, must ensue; because it is by the collocation of all the causes of the jar, for instance, that the characteristic of being an appearance belongs to its appearance. For, otherwise, the same faults would ensue also on your own theory of creation *de novo* which would equally imply the creation of a creation, and so on *ad infinitum.**

And so it is the series of all previous appearances and disappearances

*I give a translation of my pandit friend's clear note on this hard passage.

An opponent might thus argue: "But if you accept the idea of 'manifestation' and reject that of 'production,' is your manifestation itself continuous or occasional? If it is continuous, why should it not be eternal? If it is occasional, then the manifestation of this said manifestation will be either continuous or occasional. But if it is continuous, you will again have to concede that it is eternal; or if it is occasional, you will have again to show a manifestation of this occasional, manifestation, and so on. Thus you will be involved in the fault of an '*ad infinitum regression!*' Or, on the other hand, if, in order to avoid this fault, you allow that the second or third manifestation was produced, not manifested, you will be involved in the fault of 'cumbrousness,' because if the idea of production is to be conceded at all, it might as well be allowed at the very first step.

We however reply:

"We grant that if we accept the idea that a pot's manifestation was itself manifested, and then went on to concede a further manifestation of this second manifestation, we should be involved in one of the two faults you allege; but we do not concede this. We hold indeed that the pot is manifested, not produced; but we do not allow a second separate manifestation; we maintain that this manifestation of the manifestation is only another expression for the total of the causes which are said, in your phraseology, to produce the effect, the pot; is wherever this sum total is found, the manifestation takes place. This explanation removes a fear of an '*ad infinitum regression,*' as there is no continued succession of supposed manifestations.

"Nor, again, is your own hypothesis of production a whit more free from the same charge. For we may in turn ask you whether this 'production' of yours is continuous or occasional. If it is continuous, then why is it not eternal? If it is occasional, we ask, whether there is a production of this production or not? and so on, thus involving either an '*ad infinitum regression*', or the fault of 'combrousness.' And you will similarly have to same as we did, that the production of the first production is not something separate but is my another expression for the sum total of the cause, as in our case."—Cowell of the jar, for example, that is called its 'antecedent non-existence'; it is its disappearance that is called its "destruction" (or emergent non-existence); and this (destruction) sometimes becomes final also, as in the case of the body of Devadatta, or as in the case of the intelligences, etc., of those that have attained *mukti.* And what are called 'mutual non-existence' and 'absolute non-existence' are, on the other hand, really nothing but respectively the possession of mutually contradictory attributes and the site (where the thing in question might have been but is not); as, otherwise, we should have to admit another non-existence in the first non-existence, and so on *ad infinitum.** But in a cosmic dissolution there is merely the non-existence of any change of form other than and in addition to the change of form called cosmic dissolution. The *saṃskāras,* latent influences, impressions, or tendencies, arising from past acts, however, persist in subtile forms; and to this there can be no objection (and these developing as causes of future births and experiences make subsequent creations necessary).

Thus closes the investigation of Devotion under three heads (viz., Devotion, its Means, and the Object of Worship).—8

Clothed in yellow garments, resembling the (dark blue) cloud (in the colour of the body),
With long eyes like the petals of a lotus,
Holding the flute, adorned all over the body with the dust raised by the cows coming home at dusk,
May that Effulgence bedecked with the Kaustubha gem abide in your hearts.

*My pandit friend thus explains this passage: "Mutual non-existence is not something distinct, but only the possession of mutually exclusive properties. Thus 'a pot is not cloth,' 'a cloth is not a pot;' we have here an example of mutual non-existence. Now the pot has those qualities constituting pot-hood (*ghaṭatva*) which are contrary to whose which exist in cloth and similarly cloth has those qualities constituting cloth-hood (*paṭatva*) which are contrary to those which exist in a pot. So too 'absolute non-existence' (as in the phrase 'a pot is not there') is not something distinct, but is really the same as the ground where the pot is not, i.e., the absence of the pot is recognised in the ground (this is the Mīmāṃsā doctrine, *Siddhānta Muktāvalī,* p. 9). This has been accepted in order to avoid the necessity of allowing an infinite succession of absences. For as we must allow that there is no pot in the absence of a pot, we must perforce concede that there is the pot's absence in this aforesaid absence and if this second absence be something existing by itself, a third absence of the pot with similarly have to be conceded as existing in it, and so on *ad infinitum.* Hence we maintain that the absence of a pot is not something existing by itself, but simply the spot of ground where we expected to find it and it was not there."—Cowell

In the bracelet of the land of Bengal, there was Viśārada renowned as a jewel on earth,
The lord of all the earth, holding the title of the overlord of all monarchs, the foremost among the wise.
From him sprang Jaleśvara the wisest, the commander of the armies of the protectors of lands.
By Svapneśvara born of his body has been made the investigation of true Devotion.

Here ends the second lecture of the third chapter in the commentary or the One Hundred Aphorisms of Śāṇḍilya composed by the most learned teacher Svapneśvara.

Here also ends the chapter.

Completed is this investigation of Devotion.

Index of Aphorisms

Index of Subjects